*This book is dedicated to Jawaher Abu Ra
one of the interviewees. Jawaher died in 2
fired by Israeli forces at a demonstration
village.*

*We would also like to dedicate our work to all of the other Palestinian
women who have died in the anti-colonial struggle against the Israeli
occupation.*

Any profits that Shoal Collective makes from the sales of this
book will be donated to grassroots Palestinian organisations
chosen by the interviewees.

These organisations include:

- Adalah
- Human Rights Defenders
- Grassroots Al-Quds
- Al-Haq
- Jordan Valley Solidarity
- A women's project in the village of Burin
- A project bringing together children from six communities in
  the West Bank and collating their experiences for a book
- The Baladna fund for the detainees arrested during the May
  2021 Palestinian uprising

Interviews with Radical Palestinian Women

Edited by Shoal Collective
Published by Active Distribution
Page layout & design by Eliza Egret

First printed September 2021

This book is a Shoal Collective project. Shoal is an independent co-operative of writers and researchers. We produce news articles, investigations, analysis and theory-based writing as a contribution to, and a resource for, movements that are attempting to bring about social and political change.

We run the Corporate Occupation website, which tracks corporate complicity in Israeli colonisation, militarism and apartheid.

shoalcollective.org
@ShoalCollective

corporateoccupation.org
@CorpOcc

Cover photo: A Palestinian woman throws stones during clashes with Israeli forces in Bethlehem. The clashes took place after the funeral of Mutaz Ibrahim Zawahreh, who lived in Dheisheh refugee camp. Mutaz had been shot dead by Israeli forces. Photo by Anne Paq, Active Stills.

Contents

Introduction

The idea for this book came out of a concern that solidarity movements have a tendency only to engage with Palestinians about their fight against the Israeli occupation. Sometimes this can be a barrier to seeing them as fellow revolutionaries, and as comrades in our intersecting struggles for a better world and against authoritarianism, white supremacy, patriarchy, capitalism and state control.

The interviews in this book describe experiences of living under occupation, under siege, and within the Palestinian diaspora. These experiences shape how the women see the world as radicals. In talking about the Palestinian anti-colonial struggle, many of the women critique the authoritarian nature of the Palestinian Authority, and demand a liberation which deals with the many layers of oppression that they face.

The interviews also describe the struggle of being a female radical within Palestinian society. According to Mona Al-Farra: *"In the Palestinian case we all suffer from the occupation, males and females. But the female suffering is doubled due to social and traditional constraints"*. And in Lina Nabulsy's words: *"As a woman, you have to do everything that a man does, and more to get accepted. I would usually be called the 'sister of the men', or that I was 'as strong as a man'."* Lina concludes that the fight for a new society *"has to be led by women"*.

The interviewees talk about diverse subjects, such as radical, queer and ecological organising in Palestine, and their hopes for revolutionary transformation. We hope that the breadth of topics covered in the interviews will help people outside Palestine to understand the Palestinian struggle in a three-dimensional way, and to see Palestinian radicals as allies in our global struggles for freedom.

In carrying out these interviews we are conscious that our experiences as European radicals have shaped the questions that we asked. We are acutely aware that some of the terminology we used in our questions – words like 'anarchism' and 'feminism', for example – are not the terms that some of our Palestinian comrades would use to describe their politics. We often felt that we were bringing our own interpretation of what it means to be 'radical', and that this was a barrier to communicating about the underlying essence of our politics. We think that, despite these obstacles, the interviews remain illuminating and valuable.

Of course, another big obstacle we had was language. The majority of these interviews were carried out in English, which was not a mother tongue for the majority of the women we interviewed. A few were carried out with the help of translators.

We have tried to make the book as accessible as possible, and when terms have come up that our readers may not be familiar with we have explained them in square brackets and footnotes. We have also provided a simple timeline of events, as well as a glossary of terminology, at the back of the book.

We want to thank all of the women for their time and their honesty. All of our interviewees have taken a personal risk by expressing their political views so frankly, and we hope that the book does justice to their courage in the face of oppression.

Lina Nabulsy
Bethlehem, West Bank

We interviewed Lina Nabulsy (a pseudonym) in a restaurant in Bethlehem in the summer of 2018. In the weeks before our interview popular demonstrations had taken place in the West Bank against the Palestinian Authority.

Can you tell us about how you were first politicised?

I just woke up one day and there was an occupation, there were soldiers on the streets.

I grew up with the occupation. My mum tried to protect us, me and my sisters, to make sure that we didn't get into politics, but it didn't work.

During the Second Intifada [which began in 2000] things started to become clearer to me. Before that I was trying to understand what was going on. I still had a glimmer of hope and it was the era of [the] Oslo ['peace process']. After Oslo, when they started putting checkpoints in our town, I saw that something was really wrong.

During the Intifada I went to throw rocks at the Israeli soldiers. But I was never a good aim and I ended up hitting the shebab [the other demonstrators]. So instead I helped by carrying buckets of rocks to the frontlines.

At that time I was arrested and beaten by the Israelis. I had just turned 16. I was grabbed by a plain-clothes police officer and then Special Forces beat the shit out of me with batons – I was pinned on the floor for half an hour. Afterwards, I was traumatised.

They couldn't hold me because I was underage and covered in bruises. Instead, they made me sign a piece of paper to say that I wouldn't complain that I had been beaten up. I was given conditions not to be in the vicinity of Jerusalem.

Later on, I got more involved in student [political] organising.

What was it like to be a woman organiser during the Second Intifada?

At that time the space was more open for women than it is now. Society has become much more conservative since. There has been so much killing and death that religion becomes the only thing that people can hold onto.

As a woman, you have to do everything that a man does, and more, to get accepted. I would usually be called the 'sister of the men', or that I was 'as strong as a man'. You have to be manly for them to respect you. I had to be strong in front of people.

But because of women's place in the struggle against the Israeli occupation, we were given much more freedom than in other places. Because of that women are better off here than in other Arab countries.

Can you tell us about the effect of the 2011 Middle Eastern and North African uprisings in Palestine?

The revolutions happening in the Arab world awakened the desire in Palestine to stand up and shout. Palestinian women felt that this was our time to scream too.

During the Second Intifada the streets had been our space and we did what we wanted. But during the uprisings in Tunisia and Egypt we got a wake-up call that the Palestinian Authority (PA) was against us.

During the Tahrir Square protests in Egypt, the [Palestinian] police began stopping us in Ramallah [in the West Bank] and asking to see our permits. They started to increase the pressure on us, and I started to become more aware of the role of the PA.

We had forgotten how the PA, and the system itself, had been transformed since Arafat. The institutionalisation of capitalism began after [the death of Yasser] Arafat. Arafat was still a revolutionary. He never took off his revolutionary clothes. Nothing was institutionalised and he was paying people in suitcases full of cash. There was still a sense of revolution.

Arafat had an iron fist against his opponents, but it was nothing compared to Abu Mazen. They [the US] brought Salam Fayyad to power, that World Bank motherfucker,* and his mandate was to basically end 'corruption' and create institutions.

Then we started seeing that more and more of the government budget was going toward 'security'. I realised that police were getting trained to fight against their own people.

---

*Salam Fayyad was Prime Minister of the Palestinian Authority between 2007 and 2013. He had previously worked for the IMF and World Bank. Fayyad's career in the PA had been strongly backed by the US and EU.

Soldiers were getting trained in protest dispersal. Our security forces were getting trained by Americans and Europeans.

The influx of loans began. Everyone with a car in Ramallah has had a loan, which means people are tied to the system now. European funding has destroyed the essence of the Palestinian grassroots.

We used to have Popular Committees that would cooperate with each other. We didn't rely on the mercy of America and Europe. But now we are slaves to government funding. If the US decides tomorrow to stop funding the PA, then it will be shattered in a few months. This was the work of Fayyad.*

Can you tell us about women's role in the anti-PA demonstrations in Palestine since the Middle Eastern and North African uprisings of 2011?

I feel that after the March 15 2011 protests against the Palestinian Authority, we reclaimed a space for women that had been missing since the Second Intifada.

We started having debates as activists – what kind of liberation do we want? If this is what I am going to get then I don't want it. I don't want to fight for another capitalist form of a colony. I don't want the democracy that they're talking about. I don't want an Arab state like Egypt. I don't want to live in a place where I'm not free as a woman. We started to ask a lot of questions like this. It's not just about ending the occupation. It's much more global than that.

---

*Since this interview was carried out the Trump Administration drastically cut US aid to the Palestinian Authority. At the time of writing, the Biden administration is pledging to restart US cooperation with the PA.

During the 2011 protests, both Hamas in Gaza, and Fatah here in the West Bank, did everything they could to destroy our movement.

Here in Ramallah the protests got crushed by the PA. They targeted us and went after us individually, isolating us from each other. There was coordination between the Palestinian and Israeli security forces to get activists. [Later on] my friend Basil Al Araj was tortured by the PA, and then released so that the Israelis could assassinate him.*

Female activists involved in the movement were branded as 'whores on the streets of the headquarters of the president'.

When I was arrested and taken into custody by the PA I saw people bleeding, being tortured. You get tortured first in the Palestinian prisons, and then your forced confessions get used by the Israelis. Often, you get released from the Palestinian jail, then soon after you are arrested by the Israelis. There is coordination between them through the DCO [District Coordinating Office – an institution created during the Oslo agreements].

*Basil Al Araj was a well-known youth organiser and writer from the village of Al Walaja, committed to reigniting the struggle for the liberation of Palestine. He was imprisoned by the PA for six months in 2016 with five of his comrades. PA President Mahmoud Abbas boasted at the time that their arrest was an example of PA-Israeli cooperation.

The six men were held without charge by the PA, and only released after a hunger strike. Four of Basil's comrades were soon detained by Israeli forces and held without charge in administrative detention. Basil went underground for a year, but was killed after a gunfight with Israeli soldiers in 2017. See https://electronicintifada.net/blogs/charlotte-silver/why-mahmoud-abbas-boasting-jailing-palestines-youth and https://samidoun.net/2017/03/thousands-of-palestinians-join-funeral-of-resistance-for-basil-al-araj/

Torture is legal in Israel.* But in Israel you wouldn't get tortured badly for a comment you made on Facebook. You wouldn't get whipped or hung from your feet.

If we get rid of the occupation tomorrow then our next target should be the Palestinian Authority.

What happened to the protesters in Gaza?

The protesters in Gaza were calling for the same things as us. And they were crushed too, by Hamas. In Gaza they are suffocated. Hamas know who you are, they know your family.

---

*Torture was completely legal and widespread in Israeli custody from the start of the occupation. The use of torture was limited somewhat in 1999. Israeli human rights group B'Tselem writes:

"In September 1999, following a series of petitions filed by human rights organizations and by Palestinians interrogated by the ISA [the Israel Security Agency], Israel's High Court of Justice (HCJ) ruled that Israeli law does not empower ISA interrogators to use physical means in interrogation. The justices ruled that the specific methods discussed in the petitions – including painful binding, shaking, placing a sack on a person's head for prolonged periods of time and sleep deprivation – were unlawful. However, they also held that ISA agents who exceed their authority and use "physical pressure" may not necessarily bear criminal responsibility for their actions, if they are later found to have used these methods in a "ticking bomb" case, based on the "necessity defense". Following this ruling, reports of torture and ill-treatment in ISA interrogations did drop. However, ISA agents continued to use interrogation methods that constitute abuse and even torture, relying on the court's recognition of the "ticking bomb" exception. These methods were not limited to exceptional cases and quickly became standard interrogation policy." See https://www.btselem.org/torture

These modest limits on the use of torture in Israeli custody create an added incentive for Israel to outsource the torture of Palestinian prisoners to the PA.

And what about the summer 2018 protests?

After 2011, the protests continued [against the PA's policies] and they grew, leading up to what's happening now. The [anti-PA] demonstration in Ramallah [in 2018] was considered a big protest. The demands were for an end to the sanctions on Gaza. It's very difficult to believe that the PA is participating openly [in the siege of Gaza] and they have no shame in saying that they're blocking the salaries of the people in Gaza. Salaries that are coming from outside, from the EU and Arab states.

They [the PA] are also letting people die. They have stopped medical transfers [of patients between the West Bank and Gaza].

The repression of the protest was a show of force. To show us what they can do. It's a little taste of what would happen if people dare to continue to shout, and to say "no". The violence didn't come as a a shock for me, but for other people it was a surprise. Protesters were beaten, electric-shock batons were used on the street. They used tear gas, stun grenades. All of them are weapons that the Israelis use on us too.

40 people were arrested on that day. Many people who are from Fatah, and who are part of the PA, knew it was wrong. But the security forces are the ones running the show.

The best scenario for the Israelis is to have a Palestinian security force strong enough to maintain the situation as it is. That's what the security forces have been brainwashed for over the last ten years.

Is there any democracy here in the West Bank?

There are no elections, so we don't have any form of choice. The last election was in 2006.* What Abbas did [in ousting Hamas from the West Bank in 2007] was not called a coup [in the public narrative]. But the reality is that he is a dictator that completely took over the Authority, and kicked out his [Hamas] opponents that won an election fair and square.

There isn't any elected body that's currently in control of anything in the PA. It's run fully dictatorship-style, with the president who makes the decisions. The Prime Minister takes unilateral decisions as well. The three heads of security forces are the people that run the show – the Head of Intelligence, the Head of the Preventative Security Forces, and the people who are in coordination with the Israelis – the DCO. Israel needs this situation to keep us under control. The most important person for both the Americans and the Israelis is the person who controls the PA's security forces.

How should people outside Palestine view the Palestinian Authority?

Many people outside of Palestine still think that the Embassy represents us. But there is no such thing as the Palestine Liberation Organisation any more. Its institutions have collapsed.

The PA is more destructive for the struggle right now than anything else. They try to destroy the [Boycott, Divestment and

*As of 2021, talks have restarted for elections in the West Bank and Gaza.

Sanctions] BDS movement. They put on galas instead of fighting for human rights, and they're hopeless at everything.

People internationally should put the same pressure on the PA as they do the Israeli government. If people want to end injustice, then we must also end injustice of the PA. It doesn't matter if it's an Israeli or Palestinian soldier beating you, the results are the same.

Can you talk more about European funding?

When it comes to funding, everybody talks about sustainability and democracy, and they come here and give workshops to the 'natives' about the joy of democracy and gender equality. These are good topics if you're talking in luxurious Switzerland. But here the women are kept down by many layers of oppression.

The funders don't deal with the occupation. For example, they talk about the problem of water but they work around the occupation and they won't talk about the core problem, which is that Israel steals our water.

The EU gives caravans to the people of the Jordan Valley, and then when the Israelis come and bulldoze them there is no political will to do anything about it. Fuck them and their caravans!

People censor themselves in their grant applications so that they get the funding.

Instead of catering to what people need, it's catering to what the white man says we need.

If you call for BDS then you aren't going to get funding. With the American funders you have to sign an 'anti-terror' clause before you even receive a grant. You have to submit to torture in order to get the carrot.

It's a system of control. And we are losing the essence of what these organisations should be working for. It has created a bubble of very rich NGO workers, both foreign and Palestinian. A class of rich people in Ramallah, pretending to give aid.

I have never seen the gap between the poor and the middle class as big as it is now. There are women in the streets begging for money.

But the main recipient of outside funding is the PA. And it is used for training security who throw tear gas at protesters. Israeli soldiers raid our cities each night, but the PA does not stop them. If our soldiers and police can't protect the people then why are they here?

The moment Israeli jeeps arrive in Palestinian territory, all Palestinian police and security are under orders to retreat to their buildings. They're not allowed on the streets. The only reason the Palestinian police are here is to maintain the occupation. The scary thing is that these people working for the PA security forces are our neighbours.

Can you talk more about the PA's attacks on people in the refugee camps?

For the PA to be completely in control they need to control the camps, to break the autonomy of the people who live there. They have used many different tactics to do this.

Before the creation of the PA, the camps were where the leadership of the fighters would come from. During the Second Intifada [after the PA had been created during the Oslo period] the refugee camps were still fighting. And today, the weapons are still in the refugee camps.

The PA has 'Combined Committees', which are responsible for 'fighting the outlaws' [i.e. the autonomous people still resisting in the camps] in different areas. They have tried to dehumanise the people too. The reputation of the people who live in the refugee camps has changed from 'the glorious fighters', 'the revolutionaries', to 'outlaws'. Unemployment rates have gone crazy in the camps because there's a stigma about employing people.

The PA security forces go into the camps and do raids. They try and get people, but if they can't do it the Israelis do. The level of aggression against people in the refugee camps is one hundred times more than what other West Bank Palestinians face. The majority of people arrested and beaten are from Fatah; they are painted as supporters of Dahlan,* Abbas's rival. But many of them are not.

Can you talk about the co-option of resistance by the PA?

The Popular Struggle Coordination Committee (PSCC) and the Ministry of Resistance to the Wall and Colonies are both

---

*Mohammed Dahlan is a former member of the Central Committee of Fatah, and a former PA Head of Preventative Security. He was expelled from Fatah in 2011 and has since been accused of poisoning Yasser Arafat. He is still influential on Palestinian politics from his home in exile in UAE. See, for example, http://www.palestinechronicle.com/mahmoud-abbas-vs-mohammed-dahlan-the-showdown-begins/

instruments of the PA.* Grassroots activists tried to get involved, but they have basically been more destructive to the non-violent resistance than anything else. They got corrupted by money. Where does this money evaporate to?

How do you feel about the BDS movement?

BDS is the most important thing for me. I would love to see things move from the inside out. it's very difficult for us inside [Palestine] to change things. We can only beat them with resilience, and fight for our values within a society that's collapsing. To fight for love and for good.

I am fighting to keep what I love in Palestine. I'm fighting for freedom, for equality between people. Fighting to maintain myself morally. The struggle is global and not local. When we need to scream 'stop' we do. But for people outside Palestine there is more freedom for people to shout, more freedom for people to put pressure on Israel, to call for boycott.

Israel is trying hard to stop BDS. They're using all their might to fight BDS internally and externally.

---

*The Popular Struggle Coordination Committee (PSCC) is an umbrella body of representatives of the grassroots Popular Resistance Committees. Many Palestinians, however, see the PSCC as an undemocratic body, set up to bring the popular resistance in line with the aims of Fatah and the PA.

The Ministry of Resistance to the Wall and Colonies is part of the Palestinian Authority. It has played a direct role in popular resistance. For example, during the 2018 struggle against the demolition of the village of Khan Al Ahmar, the Ministry paid for buses to the protests and provided food to those resisting the evictions. Many Palestinians critiqued the Ministry for monopolising the resistance and dominating the narrative.

There are so many moral reasons to fight Israel beyond just justice for Palestine. The same weapons used against us in Palestine will be soon used against our comrades in Europe. The space is shrinking everywhere around the world for speaking out. If we don't fight then we don't have a chance to survive the storms that are ahead.

Can you tell us a bit about what motivates you to go on struggling?

For me the struggle is the same here in Palestine as for the Black Panthers. We are fighting one evil in this world. The thing that makes me a revolutionary is injustice.

We draw inspiration from freedom movements from around the world. Black Lives Matter is something that is close to my heart. The Zapatista movement [in Mexico], and watching the women rise up in Egypt and in Syria makes me stand stronger.

Our struggle has to be global. A struggle against capitalism and against patriarchy. Women need to be in charge. Men have destroyed everything. Those that create life are the ones enslaved, and are not in power. The only way is for women globally to take over completely in all aspects of life. But not women like Theresa May, Hillary Clinton or [Israeli politician] Ayelet Shaked.

Good men should support us as we're fighting together for a free world. But the struggle has to be led by women.

What kind of world would you like to see?

For Palestine, and all around the world I would like to see a place where we're allowed to live life. I want a completely different world. I want liberation. A world where respect is returned to humanity in all forms and colours. Where people are allowed to be who they are without living in fear.

I don't care what they label this place. I don't care about flags. Freedom without nationality and identity. Not the communist type or the Islamic type. I want a place where everyone of any religion is respected. Animals have to be free as well. I want utopia and I won't accept anything less.

If we die in the process of fighting for this world, then at least we have died fighting the good fight. The moment we stop believing we can get to this utopia then we don't have anything left to fight for. Why would you take another breath if you didn't believe anything can change?

Governments kill our hopes. They make us live like rats in offices, digging in holes and searching for money. Part of the way they destroy us is to take away our hopes. But the reality is that miracles happen every day.

People need to realise that there is nothing left, no hope for our children, if we don't fight. The planet is screaming "enough, I'm done". Soon the water will disappear here, and we will all be fighting in this region for water. Nature has been occupied and killed.

Maybe when people feel desperate enough we will move together globally. Why not have global protests shouting that we've had enough. Scream "hallas!" [stop!/enough!]. If I can't live a dignified life it's not worth living.

Armies live in fear. If you eliminate the fear then the soldiers will turn around and join us. The idea that we are all one can eliminate that fear. And if one of us is still in prison, then none of us are free.

Sireen Khudairy
Dheisheh refugee camp, West Bank

We carried out this interview with Sireen at her house in Dheisheh refugee camp in Bethlehem. The night before the interview took place Sireen took us to walk around the camp. That night a wedding was taking place and many people were in the streets talking and dancing.

Dheisheh is one of the places where the spirit of resistance is strongest in Palestine. It is a camp which was established in 1949 to house refugees from the villages that had been ethnically cleansed by the Zionist forces. Its walls are covered in murals showing pictures of keys (representing the keys to lost homes that the refugees had carried with them); the names of the villages destroyed by the Zionist invaders; lines of poems by Mahmoud Darwish and a picture of Leila Khaled, the communist guerilla who helped the Popular Front for the Liberation of Palestine (PFLP) hijack a plane in the 1960s.

At the time of our interview, in the summer of 2018, Israeli soldiers had been carrying out incessant night raids on the camp, detaining and blindfolding whoever they found on the streets and battling stone-throwing youths with tear gas and live ammunition. Just weeks before we visited, a 15 year old boy called Thaer Mazhar had been shot dead by the army in the streets close to Sireen's house.

Sireen is from the northern West Bank town of Tubas, and her family own land in the north of the Jordan Valley. Throughout her life she has been an organiser against the colonisation of the Valley.

Sireen came to live in Dheisheh in 2015 after meeting her husband, Mahmoud.

Can you tell us about your youth?

I was born in 1987 during the First Intifada [the name given for the popular uprising that took place in Palestine from 1987 to 1991] and grew up in the town of Tubas which is close to the north of the Jordan Valley. Lots of people in Tubas own land in the Jordan Valley and work there as farmers, agricultural labourers or shepherds.

Before 1967, people used to go from Tubas to their land in the Jordan Valley by walking through the mountains. Now they have to go through a checkpoint – sometimes it's open and sometimes not. The soldiers search people and it's a problem for the farmers because they have to wait with their fresh produce at the checkpoints, sometimes for hours.

During the Second Intifada – from 2000-2005 – it was hard to go into the Jordan Valley [without a permit]. During that time we used to walk around the Al-Hamra checkpoint [in defiance of the Israeli restrictions]. It's Israeli policy to separate the Palestinian people [in the West Bank] from the Valley.
My family has land in Bardala, planted with guava. My dad used to live in Bardala, but in the past there were no schools in the Jordan Valley so he took the easier solution and decided to

move, which is what the occupation wanted. When I got older I wondered why people had taken the easier way out and moved away.

[When I was young] I went to visit a relative in Al-Maleh in the north of the Jordan Valley. It was the first time I had been there. I returned home feeling totally sick. The people in Al-Maleh didn't have water or electricity. They lived in a very bad situation. After that, I started to ask my father more about the situation in the Jordan Valley. I was thirteen years old then. He explained to me then about Area C.* I complained to my parents, "why did you hide your experiences of life in the Jordan Valley from us? Why did you wait til I asked you about the real situation there before you explained it to me?"

I started going out to join demonstrations when I was 14 years old. It was during the Second Intifada, in Tubas. We weren't allowed to join the demonstrations during school time, but we used to skip school so we could go. The army used to attack the demonstrations, and shoot at us.

The Intifada gave me the opportunity to meet and talk to people. The experience of the demonstrations – which involved both men and women – made me start to think a lot.

When I was fifteen years old, me and my friend led a demonstration. She had received a note from a friend of hers

---

*The majority of the Valley was designated Area C under the 1993 Oslo Accords, meaning that the area would be under Israeli control until the establishment of a Palestinian state. Of course, the Israeli state never allowed the formation of a Palestinian state, but Area C remained as a zone of control. Since then Israel has forbidden Palestinians from building any structures in Area C, or from developing water or electric infrastructure. The occupation forces bulldoze anything which Palestinians build.

during class saying that her brother had just been killed. The teachers tried to calm her and say that she couldn't be certain it was true, but we ignored the teachers and left the class. We went and asked other students if they wanted to come and protest with us.

When we arrived at Al-Hamra checkpoint [which leads to the Jordan Valley] my friend's brother's body was still there. He was 22 and had been shot. We had to walk from Tamoun to Ras Al-Ahmar in order to to go down to demonstrate. They shot at us and threw sound bombs, and one person was injured by live bullets.

My father was happy that I began to be political but my mother was very worried. She supported me and said that I should do what I believed, but she asked me to be careful.

Many people used to criticise me at that time, and say things like, "Sireen has nothing to do in her life, that's why she is joining the demonstrations". The criticisms came from both men and women. Some people had respect for me, but most people didn't respect me, because I was female.

Since coming to Dheisheh I haven't experienced attitudes like this. Here men and women do activities together and support each other. But in Tubas it's totally different.

In 2005 I got involved in Jordan Valley Solidarity (JVS) [a Palestinian campaign against the Israeli colonisation of the Valley]. I joined them to help with translation and it was an opportunity for me to learn more from the people. I did tours for internationals who had come in solidarity and I worked as a project coordinator.

The main goal of Jordan Valley Solidarity is to support the existence of people in the Jordan Valley through different activities; for example, through rebuilding houses [that have been demolished by the occupation]. We managed to build five different schools and five health centres in Area C and we laid water pipes into three different communities.

You were arrested by Israeli occupation forces. Can you tell us what happened?

In 2013, on the anniversary of the Nakba [the Palestinian name for the ethnic cleansing of 1947-9, meaning 'catastrophe'], I was arrested.

The arrest was a big surprise. I was on my way back from university. A flying military checkpoint* had been set up in Tubas and they stopped my car and the other cars on the road. I was feeling fine, not expecting anything. They demanded our IDs, and then they asked me to get out of the car. After 15 minutes an officer said to me, "you are arrested". He bound my hands and blindfolded me. I asked him if he had an official paper [authorising my arrest], but he refused to answer.

Later, youths who were on the mountains above us started to throw stones at the checkpoint. The officer put me in front of him and put his gun on my shoulder and started shooting at the stone throwers with the gun balanced on me. He was using me as a human shield. It was so scary. For two weeks afterwards I wasn't able to hear properly.

Then they took me to a military base – I guess – I'm not sure as I

*Flying checkpoints are temporary roadblocks, set up to control Palestinian people's movement, or to detain people.

was blindfolded. I could only see lots of Israeli feet and shoes on the ground beneath my eyes. They arrested me at 2pm and they kept me in the military base on a tiny concrete bench for hours. I wasn't allowed to drink anything or to go to the toilet. Each time the soldiers passed me, they came close to my ear, shouted at me and prepared their weapons as if they were going to shoot.

They took me from the military base at around 2am. Then they put me on a bus full of soldiers, still blindfolded, but I could see a little from the bottom of the blindfold. It was scary on the bus with those soldiers and their shouting. They were saying bad words to me, and calling me "Arab". Saying "Arabs are animals" and "you are just an Arab woman". Another soldier said "Arab women are very cheap. If I wanted I could sleep with you."

An Israeli captain for Tubas area came to me and said, "we are on our way to your parents' house. I want you to tell us where your personal stuff is, like your laptop, camera and notebook." He threatened me that if I didn't give them this stuff they would make things hard for my parents.

We arrived at my parents' house and they took two laptops, a camera, my phone and notebooks from my room. My mum asked them if she could see me but they refused. They stayed in my parents' house for around two or three hours, making a mess.

People started to throw stones at the military vehicle I was in (they didn't know that I was inside), so the army responded by shooting tear gas and live bullets. They shot one of my friends and because of that he lost four fingers.

Then they took me into isolation at Al-Jalameh prison [near Haifa, inside Israel's borders].

I was kept there for one month in a cell which was one metre wide and two metres long. There was a toilet inside. I had no window and there was only a very small orange light.

The military interrogated me for 11 hours per day, maybe more. The only way I could see the time was when they put the food under the door, and then I could see the watch on the soldier's wrist. That's the only way I could keep track of the date, and the only way that I knew it was a new day.

In the first week of my interrogation there was a big chair, which they asked me questions on for ten or eleven hours. [They plugged me into] a lie detector. And they told me that it said I was lying.

They asked me about Jordan Valley Solidarity, and whether I was in a Leftist party. They were interrogating me about my friends and family, and then questioned me more deeply, for example about the filming of a documentary called *The Last Shepherd in the Jordan Valley*. I was surprised that they knew the journalists in the film. They asked me how we had managed to meet the Israeli settlers who we had interviewed.

I demanded the right to meet with my lawyer. But they only allowed me to see him after I had been imprisoned for 40 days. Other questions that they asked were about the photos on my laptop, about what I was thinking about doing in the future, if I planned on threatening Israeli security. They were very sure that I was planning something and they wanted to know what the plan was.

They tried to make lots of pressure against me. They gave me fake news, for example that my mother had had to go to hospital after the raid on the house. They said to me that my dad had said in a newspaper that I had shamed the family.

After one month in isolation, they brought in a guy who said he was from Tubas, my home town, to the cell next to mine. There was a hole in the wall, which was supposed to be a drain for water, and we could talk through this hole. This guy said to me, "I'm really sorry but I told them about our plan to kill Israelis." When he said that I reacted in a very harsh way. I said, "what are you talking about? Which plan?" In one second the door of the cell was opened and the captain was sitting next to him to see if I was lying.

The captain said, "okay, now we trust you that you're not going to kill Israelis. Now you can take rest and tomorrow you will go to the court."

The judge in the court said to me that they have decided to send me to Hasharon prison [between Tulkarem in the occupied West Bank, and Netanya inside Israel's borders] but that before I went there, they would send me to isolation in Ashkelon prison for two days. They told me they were preparing my place in Hasharon. But actually, it was a trick to make me think that I was going to be safer, and that I would be with other Palestinian prisoners.

There was another Palestinian who they wanted me to trust, and he told me that he had a secret phone in the jail. He asked me if I wanted to talk to my mother. I decided to give him a fake phone number. When he came back and said that he had spoken to my mother I knew that he must be a spy.

Later the same man came back again and told me that "my comrades outside jail" would take care of me and that they "needed me to answer some questions" so that they could support me. The questions were about whether I was in the Popular Front for the Liberation of Palestine (PFLP). The questionnaire had a fake stamp on it that said PFLP.

I couldn't tell him that I knew he was a spy because a few months before a Palestinian man called Arafat Jaradat* had confronted a spy in prison, and [Arafat] had been killed.

I stayed in Ashkelon for one week, and then they took me back to Al-Jalameh to the same captain. He was very angry and he slapped me. There were nine people in the room surrounding me, half of them were shouting at me. Two of them were kicking my chair. This happened for about four hours. After that, they interrogated me for three more days.

Five days later I was sent to Hasharon prison.

Sireen was imprisoned for three months in total on that occasion. She was released after her family paid NIS 7,000 (€1,495) for her release. Her release was conditional on Sireen staying at her family's home. She was forbidden from using the internet, thus isolating her from all but her immediate family and preventing her from continuing her studies. She was ordered to return to court on 16th September 2013, when she was found not guilty. But the court still ordered her not to engage in any political activity for 5 years.

*See this article by Talia Ralph in MintPress to learn more about the death of Arafat Jaradat in 2013 - https://www.mintpressnews.com/arafat-jaradat-palestinian-prisoner-dies-in-israeli-jail/51292/

How did you feel when you were released from prison?

After the experience of jail I was thinking about stopping my work with JVS. I remember talking to a friend at the time, and they said to me, "the occupation could destroy your house, they could put you in prison, but something they can't destroy is your hope. If they do manage to destroy your hope that means you are occupied. If they don't manage it, you are above the occupation."

So I started studying theatre, and presenting stories through drama with the Ashtar theatre group. [Our technique is called] the 'Theatre of the Oppressed'. Our first project was to educate Palestinian youths working in the Israeli settlements in the Jordan Valley. There were seven young people, aged from 22 to 27. Most of them were working in the settlements and it was an opportunity for them to share stories about their lives, to learn theatre and to work - because we gave opportunities for people to be employees at Ashtar theatre.

Ashtar would perform a story, and then invite the audience to rewrite the story with the solution. The idea was to invite the Palestinian Authority as well, and for [the politicians] to put themselves in the place of the oppressed. We would write down the solutions that the audiences came up with, and we would organise conferences where we would talk strategically about these solutions. So it's not just about presenting stories, it's about getting solutions from people, to get ideas to build a strategy and work on it.

One positive outcome of our performances was that there was an official permit granted to open a school for five different communities in the Jordan Valley, but unfortunately the governor died before it could happen.

Sireen, you were arrested two more times, once by the Israeli occupation and once by the Palestinian Authority. What happened?

The Palestinian Authority detained me for a day in December 2013, and psychologically they treated me worse than the Israelis. Or maybe it just felt worse because I felt that they should be my people. They were talking to me like I was an enemy, saying that they "had a peace agreement with Israel", and that I should "respect this agreement".

That time I was detained in Tubas, my hometown. In Tubas it is very shameful to arrest a woman, and I think that's the reason why they didn't hold me longer. They said to me that the Israelis were "going to arrest me again soon" if I carried on [opposing the occupation] and that I should "take care of this shitty business".

In January 2014 I was arrested again by the Israeli military, in Nablus. They took me to Huwara [where there is an Israeli military base and checkpoint, just outside Nablus]. The soldiers took off my jacket and shoes and the Israeli Commander said to me that I should remember that "I was under occupation by the only democratic state in the Middle-East" and that they were going to teach me how to respect Israel. When I heard this I went crazy, and I said, "it's not democracy, it's a criminal state. You are using this 'democracy' to kick people out of their houses and make people homeless."

The commander was really angry. He told me to run. My feet were tied and my hands too. As well as my shoes, they had even taken off my socks. The ground was covered in sharp stones. The soldiers released dogs and they started to run at me.

I felt pain in my feet from stepping on the sharp stones. When the soldiers caught up with me they started hitting me on the shoulders with their weapons. When I was released most of my body was blue.

I had never been scared of dogs before, but that night I saw that the dogs were under the control of the soldiers and they were capable of anything. Since then, I'm scared if I see a dog.

Much later, I was with an international woman in the Jordan Valley, giving her a tour and explaining the situation. She didn't know much about Palestine. Suddenly I saw a dog and I was really scared. She didn't understand why I was so scared. She started to blame my culture and background. I realised that international people need to learn more about our culture. If you don't understand the people, then you can't be part of our struggle.

After the beating, they kept me under arrest for four days. They kept me in a military vehicle and took me to court twice. They didn't allow me to sleep for two days.

In fact, they had just arrested me so they could give me a beating, but I was thinking that they were going to keep me for a long time. They threatened that they could keep me for years.

After this arrest Sireen met her husband Mahmoud, and moved to Dheisheh to be with him. But before long Mahmoud was also arrested.

What happened to Mahmoud?

In 2015 I got married and moved here to Dheisheh. My

husband Mahmoud was an ex-prisoner too and, before we were married, the Israeli Captain, who was called Captain Nidal – 'Governor of Dheisheh' – threatened Mahmoud. He told Mahmoud that the two of us would never get married and stay in one house together.*

One month after we were married, me and my husband travelled to Jordan. I was planning to be part of three theatre performances there. But [the Israeli authorities] stopped us at the border for four hours. The commander came and asked to talk to Mahmoud for ten minutes. But actually they arrested him, and he was in prison for a year.

I went to Jordan and then went back to Palestine to go to his court case. They sentenced Mahmoud to one year for joining a demonstration, where they said that he threw rocks and molotovs.

Mahmoud had been in jail before, but he had been released because of [a negotiated amnesty]. They were threatening to put him back in prison for the remainder of his previous sentence. But the lawyer negotiated and luckily this didn't happen.

I had only moved to Dheisheh two months before Mahmoud

*An Arabic-speaking agent from the Israeli Shin Bet security services using the alias 'Captain Nidal' has made more than one threat to people in Dheisheh. According to a 2016 article by Nora Barrows Freedman in Electronic Intifada, Palestinian youth have testified that 'Captain Nidal' told them, "I will make all the youth of the camp disabled," "I will have all of you walking with crutches and in wheelchairs," "I will make half of you disabled, and let the other half push the wheelchairs" and "I will make all of you stand in line at the ATM waiting for your disability subsidies and assistance." Read the details at https://electronicintifada.net/content/israeli-captain-i-will-make-you-all-disabled/17821 was arrested. When Mahmoud was in prison I was living here alone. It was difficult, because I thought that any night the army could come and attack [the camp]. But I wanted to stay there to show that I would not run away. It wasn't easy to keep on living there. With each attack in Dheisheh I thought that they would come for me.

The army attack Dheisheh often. It isn't easy for them to enter Dheisheh [because of the resistance] but recently they have started to use the strategy of dressing up like Palestinan citizens and entering Dheisheh with cars that have Palestinian plates.

Whenever they're in Dheisheh you feel like you're in a war. They use sound bombs, tear gas, and shoot automatic rifles. You can hear shouting and Palestinian people being injured. [I often hear] injured people screaming in pain or pleading for an ambulance. They attack and arrest people from the street. Sometimes they detain people and blindfold them and leave them in the street for hours.

The army often comes and attacks the camp at 1 or 2am, but recently they have started coming at 5am or 6am. They want to break the resistance. Because even now the people keep resisting. Whenever the army attacks, people resist. The women throw shoes at the army when they come to attack our homes.

The Palestinian Authority's [security forces] also attack the camp and arrest people. For example, Mahmoud was in a Palestinian jail for a month and a half.

Before moving to Dheisheh I used to hear people talking about the resistance in the camp. It was my dream to visit Dheisheh. When I put my feet in Dheisheh I felt like I was a tree, and that my roots were going deep under the streets of Dheisheh. I felt for the first time that I was in a very rich place. [Although I didn't know many people] I remember hearing the voices of the people in the houses whilst I was walking on the streets and that gave me warmth. I felt close to the people there.

I like the way that the people here stand with each other. How they still feel connected to each other. For example, if someone is wanted [for arrest], even if most of the people know where he is, he feels safe. He or she could receive help from many different people. I love the way that people cooperate with each other. That's what's most touched me – that people have solidarity with each other. They support each other because they like to do it, not because they have to.

People here accepted me in to the community and they called me 'the lady of the village'. They were very excited to learn about planting trees, and what it feels like to live in a village. The key for me was to talk about the Jordan Valley. The people here are very educated, but they don't know about life in the Jordan Valley.

While I was living in Dheisheh, me and a friend decided to make an art residency in the village of Fasayil in the Jordan Valley. During the residency we visited families, sharing life, and sitting with the women, asking them what they did with their lives and what they wanted to do. In the beginning they used to answer that they did nothing. But when we went deeper, we realised that they woke up at 4am to milk hundreds of sheep, they prepared their children for school, they milked the sheep in the afternoon, they did homework for the kids. They worked from 4am til 9pm doing hard work. But for them this was 'nothing'. If there is a house demolition [by the Israeli military], the first people who take the stuff out of the house are the women. If the bulldozers come then the women still make food for their sons and daughters. They build new houses, ready to live in again. These women have power, but they don't feel that they have it. Visiting those women was like going to school, a school where we learned about the meaning of hope and power.

Another part of me and my friend's project was to show the beauty of the Jordan Valley – the birds, the space, the peacefulness, the unique plants and the mountains. In the future we want to organise a walk for women from all over Palestine so that they can hear the stories [of the people from the Valley] and their beautiful memories from the area. The activities will be led by women.

Another of our aims is to learn traditional Arabic culture through exchanging cultural experiences, through daily life. Making mud bricks [for building houses] training and planting, working in the fields.

There is a refugee camp in the Jordan Valley called Abu Al-Ajaj camp. The people who live there are the families of people who fled from their homes in 1967 [after the Israeli occupation of the West Bank]. What's happening in Abu Al-Ajaj is still an ongoing 'Nakba' ['Nakba' means 'catastophe'] . We as Palestinians should have learned from what happened to the refugees of 1948, but we didn't. It happened again in 1967. We didn't learn the lesson, either, that time. We still live in an ongoing Nakba, where the army is destroying houses and moving people from one place to another place. We should start to build connections between Dheisheh camp and Abu Al-Ajaj. To give an opportunity for people in Abu Al-Ajaj to have connections with people in Dheisheh.

We have to sit with the old people to know the real stories, to know why things are as they are, and to build strategies. At any time people can be pushed from the Jordan Valley. We need strategies to stop this.

You want to establish a women's centre in Dheisheh?

The idea of the women's centre is to make a dead place alive again. Mahmoud's family owns an old house. It's one of the oldest places in Dheisheh. Four generations of people have lived there. It belongs to Mahmoud's aunt who lives in Jordan now. We want to renovate it. In the meantime, we're having meetings as a small group of women in our houses.

When Mahmoud was in jail, he received a monthly salary from the Palestinian Authority [a monthly stipend from the PA for prisoners who have been imprisoned by the occupation]. We collected that money and decided to do this project for the community. We will call it Dar Siti ['my grandma's house'].

It will be a place for friends to stay, for studying, and a meeting place. Dar Siti will be based on the grandmother style of living, with the traditional style of sitting on the floor. And cooking in the way that our grandmothers cooked. We want to reclaim our old culture, the old ways of living. Dar Siti will be a place for activists and artists, to be more close to the community, to talk to them, and to build their work together.

The women of Dheisheh are organising social activities for the families of prisoners and martyred people, and [they're also organising] protests to support prisoners. We all try to sit and talk together about our different situations. That's really important. Women's organising is very strong in Dheisheh now.

Shahd Abusalama
Gaza, living in the UK

We interviewed Shahd in 2021 during the Coronavirus pandemic. The 29-year-old was born and raised in Palestine, in the Jabalia Refugee Camp in northern Gaza.

Shahd has lived in the UK since 2014. She lived in London for three years and then moved to Sheffield, where she is working on a PhD about Palestinian cinema at Sheffield Hallam University. Shahd is an active student organiser, and a campaigner with the BDS movement. She also dances Dabke, the traditional folk dance of Palestine.

Since 2007 Gaza has been under siege by the Israeli state. The tiny Gaza strip – which is home to more than two million Palestinians – is completely surrounded by Israeli forces, save for a tiny border with Egypt. Crossings in and out of the Strip are tightly controlled by the Erez and Rafah checkpoints.

Gaza's skies are patrolled by unpiloted drones and F16s, while the coast is controlled by Israeli gunships. Since 2007, Israel has launched constant airstrikes on the Strip, and major military campaigns have been waged against Gaza in 2009, 2012, 2014 and 2021 (after this interview took place), killing thousands. Getting out of the Strip to study abroad is no easy feat, but it is one of the ways that Palestinians from Gaza are able to interact with the rest of the world.

Shahd, why did you move to the UK?

I got a scholarship to do my master's degree at SOAS – the School of Oriental and African Studies – in London. Luckily I made it there; it was always a dream for me, ever since I was a kid, to go to the UK and study and I've made multiple attempts, even for my BA.

But during my BA the situation in Gaza wasn't [good], it was really difficult to go out. The siege was very suffocating and choking and I remember applying for scholarships and getting really close to getting my goal – my ambition – done and then the siege happened and the borders were closed in my face. I even applied for Birzeit University [in the West Bank, near Ramallah] and I couldn't even go there [because of the Israeli siege of Gaza].

Was it difficult to get a visa?

I mean, visas are difficult for people in the Global South in general, but the thing that many people don't understand is that in the case of Gaza and its unique circumstances it's probably easier to get the visa than it is to get out of Gaza. Then there's crossing the borders. This is the reason why many people in the Gaza Strip get their ambitions crushed at the doorsteps of Rafah and Erez [the border crossing points into Egypt and Israel] and many people lose their jobs [outside] just because they decide to come back [to Gaza]. They might be working outside and decide to come back for a holiday and to visit their families, and they'd end up getting stuck for months and losing their work permit and means of income.

It was 2013 when I was trying to leave, but thankfully I had two scholarships – one to Turkey and another to the UK. I managed to use the one to Turkey as a safe transit to the UK. I finally managed, after weeks and weeks of tries, to cross the border. Turkey was more tolerant in terms of students arriving late – they gave the Palestinians a sort of special condition. However, it wasn't the case with the UK so I was kind of lucky.

How did you first become involved in politics and activism?

This 'activism' is a funny term for me, because we [Palestinians] are born into a complex situation and 'activism' – what people call 'activism' – is almost a way of life for us. I was born into a politically active family. My dad was an activist and he spent a total of 15 years in Israeli jails for his membership of the Popular Front for the Liberation of Palestine (PFLP) [a revolutionary socialist political party, historically part of the Arab Nationalist Movement and later the Palestine Liberation Organisation]. All of these political parties are considered terrorists under the Israeli occupation. All my family really – men and women – were to some extent actively engaged in what was happening, but it was really a way of life, a way to overcome our feelings of helplessness. My parents were very conscious about, for example, the weekly protest in solidarity with Palestinian political prisoners that is held every Monday at the Red Cross in Gaza – we were always there every Monday, never missed it. The oppression comes to your home, comes to your neighbourhood. We grew up very aware that the situation was very oppressive and unfair, and oppression breeds resistance.

Was it similar for others your age who were growing up around you?

I think it's entrenched in the psyche of the Palestinians to reject and refuse the oppression befalling them. How people express this differs from one individual to another, but ever since I was a kid I was going to cultural centres with members of my own generation, engaging in all sorts of activities, with Palestine and our lived experiences at the heart of it. In our context there's a very blurry line between the cultural and the political, the personal and the collective, and everything somehow intersects in our reality, ever since we were kids.

For example, you ask any child [in Gaza] "where do you come from?" They don't tell you, "oh, we come from Jabalia", or "we come from Rimal", or "we come from Beit Lahia" (I'm naming neighbourhoods in Gaza). They say, "we come from Beit-Jirja", or "we come from Jaffa", or "we come from Isdud" [places that were ethnically cleansed in 1948, and now lie within Israel's borders].

Whether they acknowledge it or not, whether they're consciously aware of it or not, this answer is very political and connotes how the oppressive situation generates political awareness amongst people. Children become older than children long before their time, against their parents' wishes for them to live a more peaceful life than theirs.

In Jabalia refugee camp, I lived through what people experienced as an 'ongoing Nakba'. In 2000, when I was nine, the Second Intifada erupted, fundamentally shaping my generation's consciousness about our surrounding realities, the land, and our place in it. Before this Palestinian uprising, my parents had always tried to reassure us of our safety, with phrases like, 'the occupation does not kill children'– only adults'. On 30 September 2000, however, when the schools were on strike, I was sitting with my parents watching television, when the murder in Gaza of twelve-year-old Mohammed al-Dorra appeared on all the news bulletins. I remember my mum covering my sight in an attempt to obstruct my vision, while urging my dad to switch channels. She could not hide it for long, however, as Mohammed and the last cry of his injured father, 'mat al-walad' (my boy is killed), became icons of the new Intifada which would last the next five years.

Israeli attacks on Palestinians intensified to the extent that UNRWA [United Nations Relief and Works Agency] schools repeatedly carried out mock evacuations as a practise for all children and teachers, to be prepared in case of any future attack against schools.

My parents, like others, struggled to provide answers for the questions from me and my siblings regarding the unjust reality we were born into, and the collective lived experience made us grow up sooner than they hoped. My generation grasped the basics at an early age; we are a dispossessed and stateless people struggling for liberation under Israeli occupation. This theme dominated all our mourning and celebrations.

As well as being active around the occupation and oppression of Palestinians have you also channelled that into other issues and campaigns?

Definitely. I feel strong affinity with the Irish, Black, Kashmiri and Kurdish struggles, for example. I think for us this kind of reaction is a matter of survival; it reminds us that we are not struggling alone. It's almost an attempt to reclaim our humanity in an immensely dehumanising situation. Many people try to channel this negative energy imposed on us from these mechanisms of oppression into positive things. We understand what oppression means. We understand what it means to be singled out because of your race or because of your ethnicity or religion. We understand this very well and this doesn't come from an abstract understanding; we didn't learn it from books but from lived experiences.

What are some of the differences between political organising in the UK and when you were in Gaza?

Back in Gaza, I was active on several fronts, at community cultural centres and organisations advocating for Palestinian political prisoners and [in] BDS. As I previously said, trying to transform this experience into something positive is truly a matter of survival and so you find Palestine, despite the odds, exporting artists – internationally renowned artists, musicians, you name it – conductors, writers, intellectuals, all professions really. I think it is also because of our understanding of the urgency and the meaning of life.

Something that I felt when I came to the UK, something that always challenged me, is our different understandings of the urgency. It's like people don't seem to understand that actions they may take could be a matter of life and death, and I've always felt that I was working at a different pace from others. This made me at times feel frustrated with people being lazy or not acting proactively enough. I was always the person trying to agitate and get a statement out or get the protest organised, or something like that, and I think it's really because [other people] don't understand how almost every minute in Palestine is a matter of life and death.

It never occurred to me when I crossed the Rafah border that I wasn't going to go back, never. But then the siege even prohibited us from returning to our refugee camps. I'm a refugee; I was born a refugee and then I find myself in a completely different setting and from afar, watching my family, my loved ones, friends and everybody that I care about surviving through siege, military occupation, and apartheid and subjugated to daily forms of violence. It fucks up your mind, really. You feel powerless as you follow the news and it's just constant horror. Especially in Gaza, which Israel treats as a laboratory where they could develop innovative ways of control, applying mechanisms that were never probably used in any other context in the history of humanity – it's just incredible how normalised these extreme injustices are.

When you know the kind of reality that people live there... By the time I left, I'd survived countless wars and so I know how real the threat is. So it's like, we're not joking: when we're campaigning we're actually trying to end the material complicity and oppression, we're really trying to save more lives, more innocent lives, from falling prey to this inhumane situation.

What does rest mean for someone who is restless? What does that look like?

I struggle with the concept of self-care that is very widely used in the UK. I wonder what is self-care and mental health when oppression is continuous, you feel it under your skin. How can you actually take care of yourself if you don't take care of yourself and everybody?

I know that no-one comes out of such inhumane situations without being affected and I'm only human to be affected by such things. But we find consolation and power in solidarity, in nurturing hope, and hope is revived from these collective actions, from being confrontational against these normalised dehumanisations. I see this as care not only for the self but for the community. Sometimes I get people saying, "oh you should rest". They say it in so many different ways of course but, I don't know, how can I detach myself from what is happening? I don't know, how can you detach yourself, how can you actually rest?

How do you see your position or role as someone living outside of Palestine? Do you get to organise with other Palestinians in the UK and what are some of the challenges of being active from the outside?

The uncertainty that a Palestinian lives leaves you – as you said – restless and just unable to detach yourself from what is happening because even if you detach yourself, it follows you everywhere.

It's always beautiful to connect with anybody on the basis of defending Palestinian human rights, but especially Palestinians. In the UK, for the first time, I met people from all over Palestine. When I was in Palestine that was a dream that was almost impossible [as it is impossible for Palestinians from Gaza to visit the other parts of Palestine]. So this segregation and dispersion we have endured added another layer of attachment to other Palestinian communities across Palestine, the Arab world and globally. Apartheid structures seek to fragment the Palestinian social fabric and geography. So it's always really exciting when I connect to people from other cities or other towns and you realise how similar you are, and how we didn't need to explain ourselves to each other because it was sort of understood. Yes, we were probably [subjected] to different extremes of violence but we know that at least, suffering, exile, and the burning desire to be free unites us. These shared experiences make us connected almost immediately.

It is actually really inspirational to see Palestinians who have never been to Palestine but are very passionate about the cause, and speak Arabic almost fluently, probably in a much more perfected Palestinian accent than mine. Such encounters make me realise how the roots truly run deep. All this is just like the wonders of hope and beauty, and confirmation that the Zionist project has failed. I talk about friends like, for example, Huda Ammori [a British Palestinian who is part of the direct action group Palestine Action] – she's never been to Palestine. So many countless examples I have in mind. They have such a connection to Palestine; it's real and inspirational. The Zionist project thought that the old would die and the young would forget. They were so wrong.

How would you describe your politics? Do you find any particular labels helpful?

I'm comfortable with the word feminist and Palestinian. I would say that leftist politics are very much part of my upbringing, even before I even understood what Marxism and communism was. It's probably related to my parents being involved with the PFLP. But I think there are some values and principles you just have to agree with as long as you're a decent human. It's not a matter of left or right.

With feminism, when I was younger, I didn't understand the word very well and I was like sort of... [laughs] it's funny I was kind of resisting the word and associating it with Western things. I had this tendency to rebel against anything that is Western associated [laughs]. To this day, the pop music that we hear all the time, I see people my age singing along and they're so hyped and I'm like 'what is this song?' I still find comfort in listening to Arabic music and films after 7 years in exile. You know, I can't avoid Netflix, especially in quarantine [laughs], but I try to watch with a critical eye.

I sort of associated feminism with a Western discourse that imposes their outlook on others without considering the specific socio-political context that give women's movements in the Global South their distinctive features. We heard what happened in France against women [who wanted to wear a niqab, or veil] and how Afghanistan was invaded in the name of protecting women. All these double standards were legitimated in the name of feminism. At that time I didn't have enough maturity to understand that the problem lies in how imperial powers hijacked feminist thought to gloss over their prejudices and crimes. Now we see this enacted bluntly by an apartheid state pretending to be democratic, and even feminist, because its military service [applies to] both men and women. The paradox also applied to Israel's self-proclaimed identity as 'a democratic Jewish state', which suggests, as many Palestinian citizens of Israel argue, that it is only democratic to Jews. The term itself contradicts itself, especially when you understand how it's based on systems of settler colonialism and apartheid; 20% of [Israel's] citizens are Palestinians and they don't have the same rights as Jews and the rest of Palestinians [who aren't citizens of Israel] are either exiled or crammed in Bantustan-like enclaves.* This reality exposes the absurdity of

*Bantustans were the isolated black enclaves set up by the apartheid era government of South Africa. The isolation of Palestinian communities from each other by the state of Israel is often compared to the Bantustans.

[Zionists and Israeli politicians] who speak on behalf of justice and human rights, [concepts] which are only monopolised to certain groups and certain races. Similarly, feminism has been hijacked; the human rights discourse has been hijacked. Everything that we thought was beautiful and represented a sense of humanity is hijacked by powers that are trying to find legitimation for their actions through empty terms that are used but not enacted.

I think that this is the same problem that ran with revolutionary thoughts and ideas that our human civilisation brought to existence such as Marxism, communism and socialism; they're beautiful and yes, there might be limitations here and there but in essence they're revolutionary in the way they empowered the oppressed and advocated an alternative reality to that imposed by the exploitative capitalist class. But, the way it's practised, the way that people in power hijack those ideas, is the alarming thing.

Do you see your creative practice and dance as being linked with the politics?

I've already said it's hard to separate things; the line between the political and the cultural, the collective and the personal is very blurry in the context of Palestine. I'm really thankful that my family encouraged our engagement with these artistic means of expression since childhood. I didn't understand how much they helped me to survive, but they truly did. I was dancing Dabke probably before I started walking – this is a running joke in the family. My siblings, cousins and I joined local troops in celebration of our culture, following my mum who was a member of a Jerusalem-based troop in the 1980s. Dabke represents an expression of identity, of resistance and of pride in our cultural heritage... It has multiple meanings: its practice is also about celebrating life, joy, community and togetherness. I also found power in drawing and singing. Most of my drawings were in black and white, partially because I didn't have access to art resources. I remember one time [while I was in Gaza] an activist who knew from online that I liked drawing, brought me gifts from outside – paper, that paper that makes drawing a lot easier and more defined, special paper for drawing; we didn't have that. I was really happy. Reflecting back I realise that I sought these means of expression and healing long before I even realised how therapeutic and powerful they are as means of intervention and communication. They definitely offered an escape from that feeling of helplessness we often felt under Israeli oppression.

I'm looking from a distance now, and I realise how so many elements in our [Palestinian] culture are basically founded on community and communal solidarity - you see this in a lot of things. You see this, for example, in the folk dance of Palestine – in Dabke, and how people enact it. In funerals and festivals of freedom and things like that. And peoples' compassion with each other – I would say that capitalism still failed to make people centred on themselves in Palestine because of this collective experience and this sense of community as well. I think it's life-changing and cultivates hope and resilience. But I also know how important solidarity is in these sort of settings and how it can be really a front of resistance against such mechanisms of oppression.

When I came to the UK so many elements of my life were missing, and I was constantly nostalgic and missing this sort of dynamic life that I used to have back home. I also really believe in how meaningful it is and how expressive it is of the

Palestinian resistance and cultural heritage. The narrative of resistance is embodied in the songs, the way our bodies move and the way people come together, holding hands and dancing together, there's a lot of beauty to it. As soon as I arrived in London, one of my first questions was, 'is there a Dabke group here?' Luckily there was, a group called 'Zaytouna', as in 'olive'. They had been dancing for over 10 years, and were on the verge of collapsing due to internal tensions, so I joined them for barely a year before the group sort of dissolved.

I was still determined not to miss this element in my life. So I joined with a few women who still wanted to carry on dancing, and we formed our own women's group. We called it 'Hawiyya' (Arabic for 'ID') and we established it in 2017. We were only four women and now we're eight, so we're growing slowly but steadily and we choreograph our own performances and have travelled throughout the UK performing Dabke. We've done refreshing collaborations with Palestinian Dabke groups back home such as Lajee (Beithlehem), El-Funoun (Ramallah) and Layali Al-Farah (Gaza). The power of Dabke makes people with minimal to no knowledge about Palestine fall in love with the cause and become so curious about learning, you know it sort of instigates this curiosity from people. I think that it's really important to remind [others] that the Palestinian people are holding onto their heritage and have vibrant things to be celebrated, aside from the widespread images that associate Palestinian lives with violence.

How are you feeling now about the situation for Palestinian people and the way things are in the world at the moment? Where do you see the hope?

Sometimes I get super depressed. There are so many worrying

signs, such as the rise of the right-wing and xenophobia. I think that's also why cultivating hope is a matter of survival.

My personal experience outside Palestine raised my awareness of the surrounding net of oppressive politics and practices. After I finished my master's degree, I ended up living through the inhumane process of asylum seeking, as the doors to Gaza were still closed. That was really re-traumatising but also eye-opening to British society, and European society in general. I was campaigning for refugee rights with Women For Refugee Women, Movement for Justice, By Any Means Necessary, SOAS Goes to Calais. We grew connected with other groups campaigning for refugee rights across Europe and in Turkey. With my background of originally being born a refugee, I became very invested in this issue, hoping to save future generations from this vicious circle of violence. The scale of double standard and hypocrisy is just incredible, and we see this in Europe where the motto 'never again' originated. The targeting of other minority groups – the Muslims and Arabs and everyone who's considered 'other' – amid the rise of the right-wing policies that scapegoat these communities is really alarming and makes you wonder if any lessons have been learned.

The system is deeply complicit in perpetuating violence against the Palestinians and enabling Israeli apartheid and the crimes against us, to the extent that we feel we can never really break free of violence. Whether in Palestine or outside, all of these intersecting mechanisms of violence are chasing me wherever I go; I see them in brands, normalised on supermarket shelves, brands such as Puma [which sponsors the Israeli Football Association], banks such as HSBC [which invests in companies that arm Israel], not to mention the media discourse that shamelessly reproduces the Israeli narrative.

That's why I actively sought campaigning groups; for me those constituted windows of hope and potential change that feels more achievable when our energies unite. So, yeah there are signs of hope but I think people really need to step up to those challenges, because we are facing times like no other before. I think the pandemic uncovered some of these structural inequalities globally, and hopefully it made people more aware of how interconnected we are, or maybe I'm just feeling optimistic. I hope I'm not alone in thinking this.

I think what is happening in the Labour Party is alarming – the deliberate conflation between anti-Zionism and anti-Semitism and [between] Zionism and Judaism is really troubling, has a very chilling effect and [shows] how powerful the Zionist lobby is. Even anti-Zionist Jews are not exempt from these silencing attempts. Jeremy Corbyn once gave the impression that another form of politics that is biased to the oppressed and the poor is possible, but the organised Zionist witch-hunt and his replacement with a self-proclaimed Zionist tell us that there's still long way to go.

In one's bubble of safety and comfort, it is easy to assume that we enjoy freedom and equality, but all these are a façade, and they don't really reflect the genuine reality of things. If only people understand how they are part of enabling this system, and how their privileges could deprivilege others. Tax payers cannot be considered passive once we understand how their tax money is being invested in funds that go into the arms trade or into facilitating those mechanisms of oppression. It's the same with citizens who have the right to vote but help bring a Trump into power and uphold anti-refugee attitudes, or pro-Israel, or pro-apartheid values. The vote has a weight and if you're a responsible citizen, you shouldn't be thinking in terms of individualistic interests. At this time and age, I think it's a must that we live with open and critical eyes, because otherwise we're eaten within. First it was the Gypsies, then the disabled, then the homosexuals and then the Jews and Black people, then the Armenians and the Bosnians, and the Palestinians and the Muslims... the scapegoat will only be changing if we don't really open our eyes to stand firm for our human values and for freedom, social justice and equality for all.

I do believe in the power of people and I do believe that hopefully Palestine will have its South Africa moment. The BDS [campaign] is very, very powerful; it's growing. The fact that Israel is delegating a whole ministry to combat the BDS – The Strategic Affairs Ministry [an Israeli government ministry established to counter the success of the BDS movement], this signifies how threatened and insecure they are. The use of hard power by Israel and other states further reveals the real threats that such peaceful movements are posing. Before, the use of soft power* may have made it difficult to see, but now the police and the intelligence [agencies] are using hard power. Activists are being jailed, protesters are being [attacked] with [tear gas] canisters and even shot in the streets in places that claim to be democratic and to value human rights. We also see refugees, including Palestinians, dying at the shorelines and borders of the EU due to xenophobic policies. The use of hard power is an indication that hegemonic systems are weakened, and it's also opening people's eyes to what's really happening. If you're safe today you might not be tomorrow.

*Hard power commonly means the use of forceful power such as physical repression, invasions, arrest and imprisonment. It can also refer to the wielding of economic power such as sanctions. Soft power relates to a more subtle form of power where a state tries to put forward arguments that serve its objectives. The state of Israel's political use of false accusations of anti-semitism against BDS organisers is an example of this.

Lama Suleiman
Haifa

We met Lama at her home in Haifa. In 1948 British Mandate troops withdrew as the city came under attack by Zionist forces. The city fell, and tens of thousands of refugees fled from Haifa to Jordan, Lebanon, Syria, Egypt and elsewhere. Today the city is within the borders of the state of Israel.

Lama grew up in Nazareth. But has lived in the UK and studied in London. After returning from the UK she continued as a postgraduate student in Haifa.

We asked Lama about being a radical Palestinian feminist living inside the Israeli state.

What was your experience of attending an Israeli university?

Throughout my experience of studying in Israeli universities, I was often the only Palestinian in the programme. I encountered systemic discrimination on a daily basis, but having the privilege of getting a foreign education [in the UK] had put me at a higher level than Israeli students and enabled me to overcome the very stark educational disadvantages that limited my work and my access to knowledge.

The experience of alienation also extended to my encounters

with students and peers. I was always the Arab that didn't fit their stereotypes, but when it came to my Palestinian identity or academic work, they were at best an uncomfortable topic, and at worst, belligerently discredited by my Israeli peers for not conforming to their hegemonic narratives and values.

Can you talk about how ideas of non-hierarchy influenced you while you were at university in London?

I learnt a lot of things that have stuck with me from my experience of the anarchist movement in the UK. Especially ideas about non-hierarchy, because it helps you understand your place in a movement and your relationship to others and helps deal with the emotions that you have being part of a group.

Dealing with these emotions and ideas in a group is a strong aspect of how you can sustain deep activism and build community. It's one of the most important building blocks of creating a sustainable radical left movement.

I was quite young at the time, and I found this experience to have inspired much of my work, activism, and writing. Unfortunately, after being active in Palestine for the past 7-8 years, the difficulties, power relations, and inner tensions I have encountered within the Palestinian community in Haifa have really drained my energies.

Did this influence you when you returned to Palestine?

When I came back here, I wanted to utilise anarchist ideas and methods in the place that I know best. But I didn't really succeed, for many different reasons.

In my immediate circle in Haifa, I found that people weren't very interested in talking about group dynamics or power relations. They were mostly preoccupied with the larger context of Israeli oppression and occupation, and social hierarchies were not perceived as an important thing to struggle against. I think that's a shame, and counter-productive.

But I've always believed that things have to develop organically. I think you can learn a lot from other struggles but I don't think you can simply import ideas from other places and expect people to practise them. Yet, since the last couple of years a more radical feminist and queer discourse has been developing [in Palestine].

How would you describe your politics now?

I don't agree with using labels when talking about politics, I think politics should be a conversation. The only label I would identify with and try to live by here is the label 'feminist'. It's the most immediate and daily struggle for me.

I don't consider myself a Palestinian nationalist, but I identify as a Palestinian as an anti-colonial political identity. I [couldn't call myself] an anti-capitalist either, because I have been habituated to being a consumer.

I would consider myself to be an anarchist. Yet, while I abstain from dealing with Israeli colonial institutions, my livelihood is often dependent on the state. And although I think the parliamentary system (especially in Israel) is an illusion of democracy, sometimes voting for Palestinians can be tactical.

However, to be an anarchist, you can't live [a radical] life on your own, you need a community of people around you in order to develop.

I don't think that I live my life the way I believe in right now. I have reached a point where I have to conform to the way things are in order to get things done. There aren't many loopholes in the way of life here, you can't really escape the system. Life is too integrated into capitalism, and the Israeli state is one of the strongest capitalist systems in the Western world today, even more so than the UK.

Also, the path I have chosen, writing and researching, means I have to be in an academic framework to do it, and following that path has meant that I am integrated into the capitalist system. My daily life here is struggling to pay rent, so it doesn't leave me that much space. But I guess that's just how it is in any capitalist country.

Can you talk about people's struggle to survive financially here in Haifa?

Israel is supposedly a welfare state. It's built on the premise of a welfare state [i.e. high taxation]. But your taxes go toward paying for the military apparatus of the state and to serve the interests of corporations and wealthy sectors. The system only supports you if you're on or below the poverty line, and even then you get the bare minimum to survive so you can continue to exist in a state of perpetual poverty and debt.

The system in the UK is better able to absorb changes in the economy than here. Here there is a lot more precariousness. A lot of young people here are unemployed, and rely on temporary and precarious jobs with unlawful work and pay conditions. If they happen to be students they can't even apply for benefits from social security. There aren't [many] unions to support precarious workers.* And it is common for employers to take advantage of their workers especially because there aren't many work opportunities available to them elsewhere.

In the last two years [from 2016-18] the economy has been changing, the rents have been steadily rising, but salaries have stayed the same and are below what you need to get by. I'm now thirty-three years old with a master's degree, but I can't get a job to live or develop from.

How does Israeli capitalism intersect with Israel's colonisation of Palestine?

The Israeli settler project and the other Western colonialist projects in the Middle East were never really about nationalism. [Zionist colonialism] has been a capitalist colonial project since it began in the 1900s.

Although Palestine has historically been a capitalist society, nowadays it is reliant on the Israeli occupation and its economy, and the Palestinian Authority (PA) is in itself complicit in producing and perpetuating capitalist relations and inequalities.

Can you talk a little bit about why you don't identify as a Palestinian nationalist?

The Palestinian predicament for the last hundred years is the result of nationalism eclipsing anti-colonialism, which was a much more inclusive struggle.

*Maan (http://eng.wac-maan.org.il) is one union that does work with precarious Palestinan workers within Israel's borders.

Historically the struggle was never about Palestinian nationalism. I think Palestinian nationalism was a reaction to Zionist immigration and to the Jewish nationalist project. Palestinian nationalist discourse began as a strategic discourse to counter it. Nationalism was growing at the time. So in some ways it was the only language that people could take up. Nationalism was the only way for the Arabs in Palestine to stand their ground and claim their entitlement to their land.

The more history has unfolded, the stronger the nationalist discourse has grown . There were a lot of different ideas that we have lost along the way. A similar process happened in the UK, in Europe. Just like everywhere else, nationalism had won.

I think the turning point was the Zionist immigration [to Palestine] and the victory of the nationalist discourse. It doesn't mean that all the ideas [that came before] were lost. There are still echoes even now in certain places.

[The ethnic cleansing of] 1948 also had a significant effect in completely disconnecting what was before and what came after.

What do you think were the ideas lost along the way? Before there was nationalism, what were people's ideas?

Before the end of the Ottoman Empire, there were a lot of people talking about the decentralisation of the empire. There was talk about all of the different Arab, non-Arab, and various religious communities across the empire having equal rights, and becoming citizens of the empire. There were discussions about decentralising power from Istanbul, and for every region of the empire to have its own [autonomy].

There were Islamic discourses too, and there were also Arab nationalists, who sought to create a pan-Arab state. What is going on today in Syria with ISIS is not so detached from these two discourses. It's a continuation of what was disrupted along the way.

There was a huge spectrum of ideas. Some ideas stick, some don't.

I don't consider myself a Palestinian nationalist [at heart]. But I would think of myself a Palestinian nationalist politically speaking, in terms of how I would identify myself as in order to counter Israeli racism and colonial discourses. So it's more of a strategic thing for me.

Would you be happy to see a Palestinian state emerge?

That's a difficult question. But I don't think that there will really be a Palestinian state...

[A Palestinian state] already exists in some form and I don't think anyone really likes how it looks. So it wouldn't be a desirable state for the future.

I don't believe in a two-state solution and I don't believe that a one-state solution is possible any more. Even though the latter is the most ideal, it is already past the point where it's possible to achieve.

Personally, I think that Palestinian identity can only exist theoretically. When the Great March of Return began in Gaza [in 2018], I was closed up in my room for a few months and I was reading and writing for my research about Palestinian history. At the time, I was really detached from reality, because what I was researching was pre-1948, and it has a lot of nostalgia and magic in it.

I began thinking about the Great March of Return in Gaza, I started connecting it to what I had been reading, and I started to see that people [participating in the march] still have that nostalgic vision of Palestine, and aren't willing to let go of it. They still thought that it was a place to which they *can* return.

That realisation had a lot of sadness in it. *[The marchers]* are attached to returning to somewhere that doesn't exist any more.

Us Palestinians inside Israel know this very well. There is nothing left here. We try to symbolically say "yes! We remained in Haifa", and we are doing these cultural projects to reclaim the Palestinian heritage of the city but we know hardly any of it really exists anymore. It is only in our imaginations.

This idea that young people in Gaza were willing to die for something that deep down they know doesn't exist any more, it only goes to show the level of despair we have come to.

Here [as Palestinians living within Israel's borders] we are in denial about most things. We keep ourselves to ourselves, we try to make the most of the everyday and we try to avoid violence and immediate conflict. Try to live life normally. While in other [parts of Palestine] life is anything but normal.

But we're still really attached to this idea of Palestine. So how do you reconcile nationalism, and wanting a state, wanting to better the lives of people who have been suffering for decades -

how do you reconcile this with the fact that what they want doesn't exist any more? Maybe this way of thinking has to do with where we are. With living in Haifa, in the north, in so-called 'Historic Palestine'.

How much have you heard about the Kurdish freedom movement and the revolution in Rojava: the idea of democratic confederalism and people organising in a directly democratic way at local street level?

The Kurdish freedom movement was calling for a state. They were nationalist in the same way that Palestinian movements are. Then they began to call for a democratic confederation that wasn't a state, and they began to criticise the state and to say that states were just another form of oppression. How much do people in Palestine know about this?

I don't think people know enough about it at all. I think that the Kurdish situation is a common reference point that is similar to the Palestinian crisis in many ways. But I don't think our situations have been compared that much.

I think the Kurdish [freedom movement] today has managed to succeed to do what the Palestinians didn't. It's a good example of anti-nationalism, and that's the main difference to the Palestinian struggle.

They succeeded despite not having the privilege of having the world's attention - at least not until recently. I think we could learn a lot from that, if we would listen.

[For Palestinians] the struggle against colonialism and

capitalism is very much concentrated on the Israeli occupation. Unless we break out of that framework we won't be able accomplish much.

The world has become so woven together, I don't think that you can separate one issue from another any more.

Being occupied by Israel diverts our attention from places where we can make change . The Israeli state isn't going to collapse any time soon, it is what it is. Just like capitalism isn't going to disappear in one day. It's part of the same logic.

As long as the nationalist struggle is only focused on anti-Zionism, is just a reaction specifically against the Israeli state, then it doesn't have much potential to change the smaller things. The things that get forgotten but which are of no lesser importance.

What things do you mean specifically?

For me I think community building is crucial. I think institution building is not possible inside the Israeli state: there are too many laws against it. Although, there is much more possibility within the Palestinian state.

You talked about feminism earlier, and self identified as a feminist. Can you talk about what it's like to be a Palestinian feminist inside the Israeli state?

There's different experiences [of being a feminist] here in different frameworks. It's different if you're a Palestinian woman in an Israeli institution or, for example, a woman living in a Palestinian village, or a Palestinian woman living in an

Israeli city – these factors change your experiences greatly. And then there's also the issue of being a woman within the private sphere of the family.

For me at least, I take on different feminist identities in each of these frameworks. The most problematic sphere for me is the private sphere, where I feel I have to compromise my own values and way of life in order to keep the peace and not to insult anyone.

Whereas when I am in public I don't really care what people think, and I don't worry about the outcomes, as they don't affect me as much.

In Haifa, I can say and dress how I like because people don't know me here. In Nazareth [where my family live] it would be different and I would have to change my appearance and behaviour to adapt to the value system of the place. I would have to think twice about what I'm wearing, how I speak and where I'm going.

I don't come from a traditional family but I still encounter some situations where I'm not accepted as I am, and I am expected to change or compromise in order to please the rest of the family.

It is a choice of whether to confront or to keep the peace. It's something I have to keep thinking about, about where to draw the line between when to compromise – to keep the peace – and when I have to enter into a confrontation in order to protect my personal space or to fight for something I really want/need. It's kind of weird that after [more than] 30 years of living I'm still not used to it. Maybe someday I will be.

Could you talk about feminist organising inside the Israeli state, and in Palestinian society in general?

Well I've never been active in feminist organising in Palestine before. I think most of the feminist organisations here are traditional in the sense that they operate only within the gaps left by the Israeli state, in the places where people fall between the cracks.

In most cases feminist organising has to do with violence against women, focusing on violence in the family, honour killings, forced marriages, etc.. But I have rarely encountered organisations that work on sexual harassment in the workplace, which is one of the most prevalent problems that women encounter here on a day-to-day basis.

I think feminist organisations have the potential to grow here if they [include] women who have different kinds of experiences, to validate and affirm these experiences and difference, and to move away from discourses of victimisation.

Feminism in Palestine is not yet intersectional enough, as it does not discuss/mobilise around other issues/inequalities such as class, or queer, or racial discrimination within Palestinian society.

[Palestinian queer organisation] Al-Qaws, for example, is another progressive and radical organisation in Palestine that has been developing a very interesting queer-relevant discourse and practice. They have clear feminist overtones, but it too has not been very open to considering intersectional action.

I think that as long as different Palestinian movements and struggles remain limited to identity politics, the more time it will take us to begin to make important connections between discourses, movements, actions, and struggles.

Do you think nationalism has limited the space available for struggles against patriarchy and LGBTQI+ struggles?

Actually, I think the nationalist struggle does have space for feminist discourse and for other struggles. Both [nationalist and feminist] discourses can exist together. I think they come together quite nicely. They bring out the importance of anti-colonialism.

It's an interesting question, especially when it comes to struggles around sexuality. A friend on Facebook has recently asked a question about whether there are any stories in Palestinian folklore that mention queer sexuality. It's definitely a matter worth researching, and I am sure some have already begun doing so.

Can you talk about radical organising in Palestine?

The Palestine Liberation Organisation (PLO) was formed during the military rule [in Israel from 1948-1966] in the first two decades [after the Nakba]. But this wasn't the beginning of the Palestinian struggle; there were many significant Palestinian anti-colonial movements before that.

During the 1920s there were big Arab mobilisations here in Haifa, in Jerusalem, Nazareth, and other cities, by workers' labour unions and women's movements. It was in the context of the growing consciousness of the threat of Zionist immigration,* the ways it was affecting the Palestinian economy, agriculture, and industrial development, and the British policies that were accommodating Zionist immigration and institution building and causing a Palestinian recession.

People were also increasingly aware of the vast class inequalities within Arab society and communities in Palestine, and the ways in which rich Arab capitalists were complicit [in the oppression of the working-class], and British colonial policies in Haifa and other cities and villages.

Can you talk more about how nationalism sidelined the anti-colonial struggle?

The struggle began as an anti-colonial struggle since the late 19th century and early 20th century, but after World War II anti-colonialism and anti-capitalism became sidelined by nationalism.

The nationalist movement took form in a number of ways. Even before World War One, Palestinian nationalist movements were beginning to develop. Their development has a lot to do with 'Arab modernity'. [Arab modernity] was similar to Western modernity in the industrial sense, but culturally Arab modernity was quite different.

---

*Large scale Zionist migration to Palestine had begun in the 1880s. Immigration increased massively after the British mandate powers promised to support Zionist immigration in the Balfour Declaration of 1917. Palestine's Jewish population doubled during the 1920s, and doubled again during the 1930s. Zionist organisations such as the Jewish National Fund purchased more and more land, displacing many Palestinians. Soon, Zionist colonial militias were set up to push Palestinians off the land. Numbers increased again in response to Nazi oppression of Jewish people in Europe.

The concept of Arab modernity developed towards the end of the 19th century. The '30s and '40s were the height of Arab modernity - with the development of theatre, of photography, of political mobilisation, and feminist mobilisation. A group of Palestinians/Arabs in Palestine founded the Arab Bank.* The Arab Bank was an attempt to create an autonomous bank as an attempt for people here not to rely on foreign institutions.

Yet, the breaking up of Greater Syria also meant that modernity took different forms in Syria and Lebanon to the forms it took in Palestine.

*The Arab Bank was the first private financial institution in the Arab world. It was founded in Jerusalem in 1930. It is now headquartered in Amman, Jordan.

Faiza Abu Shamsiyah
Al-Khalil (Hebron), West Bank

Faiza is an activist and video journalist in the West Bank. She lives in Tel Rumeida, a neighbourhood of the city of Hebron which lies very close to several Israeli colonies inhabited by extremely violent settlers. Approximately 2,000 Israeli soldiers are stationed close by, ostensibly to protect the roughly 700 Israeli settlers. 21 Israeli military checkpoints are situated in and around the Old City of Hebron.

Like every Palestinian family in Tel Rumeida, Faiza's family encounters daily acts of harassment and violence from the Israeli military.

Can you tell us about yourself?

I'm a resident of Tel Rumeida in Hebron, and I'm a mother of five children. I'm an employee of the Hebron governate office. I'm also a woman activist, and a video journalist with Human Rights Defenders. I document the killing of women at the Women's Centre for Legal Aid and Counselling, a Palestinian NGO which works all over the West Bank.

I have been a video journalist since 2010. My first experience of filming was with [the] B'Tselem [human rights organisation]. After settlers attacked my daughter, B'Tselem supplied the family with cameras and I began to volunteer [with them].

My daughter was going to school earlier than normal because

she had an additional class, so she left the house at 6am. Coincidentally there were three or four settlers passing by at the same time and they set their dog on her to attack her. She ran away. While my daughter was running, she fell and broke her jaw, and she was taken to hospital. She was unconscious for two days. I met B'Tselem volunteers and they collected statements. They suggested that I take a camera.

In the beginning I refused. I said, "I cannot film." But my husband said, "take the camera and I'll train you how to use it." When I first started, sometimes my pictures weren't level and sometimes I forgot to open the lens! My husband also encouraged me not to be afraid of being attacked by the settlers.

Another trainer from B'Tselem gave us a workshop about safety whilst filming. Then I became more used to it. The camera was important, because it reduced the number of settler attacks on my family. The settlers knew we had cameras. They used to attack me and try to break my camera, try to take the memory card, and sometimes soldiers came up to me to prevent me from filming.

Every time I filmed I was restricted, but this made me stronger. Then I started going out and filming if my neighbours were attacked. Sometimes I would document the clashes [between stone-throwing Palestinians and the army] on the streets. I like using the camera to reveal the crimes of the occupation.

Can you tell us about Human Rights Defenders?

Tel Rumeida was closed in 2000, after the Second Intifada [began]. On November 1st 2015, after the assassination of

Hadeel, the closure was further emphasised and became a lot harder, with specific IDs given to the people of the neighbourhood [and everyone else banned from entering].*

[The Israeli military] prevented the media from coming into the neighbourhood. So we started filming things by ourselves and we formed Human Rights Defenders. We have around 23 Palestinians volunteering with cameras and lots of international activists. Human Rights Defenders has also trained children [to film] in schools which are close to settlers and the army. The group doesn't just film in Tel Rumeida, but [close to] the settler enclaves around Kiryat Arba.

Now people who film footage with their phones also give us their videos. And we have a group of women in Gaza who are cooperating with us too. We exchange footage and we talk about our suffering.

We have good relations with B'Tselem and sometimes we give them footage. But we felt that B'Tselem's attention on the area had decreased, and sometimes they didn't take our videos and publish them. But the coordinator of B'Tselem is still my hero and I still follow what she does.

Our main goal is to expose the crimes of the occupation and we're open to cooperating with everyone. It's become a phenomenon now – everyone holds their phone and starts filming. But with B'Tselem there we feel more protected because it's an Israeli NGO and has a big name. This gives us some protection because we work alongside them.

*In 2015, Hebron's Palestinians came under very heavy violence from the occupation after the outbreak of a new Palestinian uprising against the occupation.

If you don't praise the people who help you, you don't praise God! I have an excellent relationship with them and I talk to the B'Tselem coordinator daily.

We appreciate B'Tselem's support but we felt that a Palestinian-led body is necessary and deserves support from others. There is a difference between those who live such reality and those who observe it. We don't work 9 to 5, and what motivates our work is the spirit of belonging and survival. We know that Israeli violations are not limited to 9 to 5 on week days. Such assaults can happen at any time. If Israeli forces break into our house at 2 am, who's going to defend us? If we call B'Tselem, they would be closed, as 2 am falls outside office hours.

This is why a Palestinian-led body like the National Association of Human Rights Defenders, which the people of Tel Rumeida founded in 2017, cannot be substituted. We also noticed that much of our filming which we sent to B'Tselem would be left in their archives and never published.

Therefore, through Human Rights Defenders, we feel more empowered, we have control on our narrative and we expose our lived reality as it is, with no filters. Currently due to the pandemic and Israeli military restrictions on who enters the military zone, our relations with B'Tselem are not as strong as before. But we keep going on. We called our [first] filming project *Capturing the Occupation Camera Project*. We founded it in 2017. Another renowned Palestinian activist, Badee' Dweik, is involved.

We started with very humble means, but we were determined to do this as it was about life and death. We also did it for the sake of history, to keep things on record. The International

Solidarity Movement* branch in northern California were monumental in helping us, providing cameras and laptops to help us found HRD. Ever since, we distributed those cameras to the families of Tel Rumeida and trained children and their parents on how to use [them] in a safe and effective way. For example, we advise them to remain 25 metres away from the violent events they witness, a distance that is sometimes hard to achieve when people themselves are at the centre of the violence, but we do our best.

How is it as a woman, doing your job?

In the beginning I was worried about what people would say about me in Palestinian society. But I'm a strong woman and I have learnt to challenge everything. My neighbours started calling me if they were being attacked by settlers. Many of the women want to join us and video, but they're worried about whether the settlers will attack them. I've started encouraging them and raising their spirits.

As a Palestinian woman I try to focus more on how the children and women suffer. I also try to encourage women to go and visit the Ibrahimi mosque: they don't want to go because of the checkpoints [which surround the mosque]. I take them to eat breakfast in the old city or pray in the mosque.

Can you talk more about the hassle your family gets from the settlers and soldiers in Tel Rumeida?

Sometimes I will go and film settlers and they run away. But

*International Solidarity Movement (palsolidarity.org) was founded during the second Palestinian Intifada. It aims to support Palestinian grassroots resistance to the Israeli occupation.

sometimes they try to beat up my children or throw trash onto my house [roof], or go onto my roof and pee down onto the house. They even burnt part of my house, and they poisoned the water tanks on my roof.

One time we wanted to be sure that the water tanks were clean, and my daughter went up to check them. Five settlers came to the roof and chased her to the edge and then pushed her. On another occasion she was walking home from school and they burnt her hair. She was only seven years old at the time. She had psychological issues because of these experiences, and Médecins Sans Frontières treated her.

My youngest boy was stabbed once in his arm and this was documented on video. He was detained for four or five hours [by the military] when he was nine years old and put in complete isolation.

My oldest son, Awni, is the most harassed. In 2013, Awni was beaten. And on 22nd December 2015 he was shot in both his legs, on the hilltop in Tel Rumeida. The settlers used to target Awni [as a way] to get revenge on the whole family [for remaining in Tel Rumeida, and for their work with B'Tselem and Human Rights Defenders].

[As of April 2021] Awni is currently banned from entering the closed military zone. In early 2021, the military court issued an order to prevent Awni from entering Tel Rumeida [where the family lives], until 2023.

Madelin, my daughter, was once forced to stay indoors for fifteen days because she was directly threatened by a female settler. Another time, Madelin was detained for three hours with a couple of other girls and interrogated by the Israeli police. After that, two Israeli police officers came to our home and accused Madelin of throwing rocks at settlers. The police officers said that for her own safety she should stay indoors for two weeks.

The same thing happened [to] me in 2019. I was put under home arrest for two weeks. The whole story behind it is ridiculous. On 31 October 2019, Awni and I had just returned from Jordan; Awni had had three [operations on] his legs after he was shot by the settlers.

Some visitors [came] to check on us. [Soon after], Israeli soldiers broke into the house. Their excuse was that they had got news that some Palestinians [had been] smuggled illegally into Tel Rumeida. I stood up to challenge them and protect my son and visitors, and they arrested me and interrogated me. Eventually they accused me of 'disrupting soldiers at work' and put me under home arrest.

This is just some of [mine and] my children's suffering, but all of the families in my neighbourhood suffer, and every household has their own story.

Does having a camera with you reduce the harassment from soldiers and settlers?

If soldiers behave in a rude way, having a camera there can reduce that. The soldiers now look around and check whether people are filming. In certain incidents, the footage has shown the truth and that has helped a lot of people. We send someone to film the action. But we also send someone to film the filming, taking different angles. I know of about ten cases where the

Israelis were going to make a fraudulent claim [against Palestinians] or where [Israeli forces had] detained people. But these people were released before arrest because of the cameras filming. [In Hebron, and elsewhere in Palestine, it is common for Palestinians to be detained blindfolded on the street by Israeli soldiers, before either being arrested or released].

All these documented events are published on Human Rights Defenders' Facebook, and the YouTube channel of the *Arresting the Occupation Camera Project*. We currently have more than 2,000 hours of film of real events that we encounter and we encourage film makers and international human rights defenders to get in touch [in order to put] these filmed events [to] effective public use.

[In 2018] I was drying my laundry and one of the Israeli soldiers who were stationed on our home's rooftop started blowing me kisses. So I started filming. At the same time my son, Saleh, was coming home, and the soldier started bothering him. My son came into the house, but then the soldiers came round, saying that they wanted the boy. The same soldier who had been blowing me kisses had told his colleagues that Saleh had been throwing rocks at him. DCO officers then came, DCO stands for District Coordination Office, [which are] Israeli-Palestinian military coordination offices established as part of the 1994 Gaza-Jericho Agreement between Israel and the Palestinian Authority. I told the officers that the soldiers were coming to arrest my son, but that he didn't throw rocks. I told them that the soldier was trying to flirt and that this was against our custom. The DCO saw my footage and Saleh wasn't arrested. The soldier was told to go to the military base, and later I saw him sweeping the street. He came and apologised to me, saying that he'd thought he had been greeting me, not flirting. The DCO said that I could complain to the police, although I haven't. This is life for Palestinian women under the occupation.

In March 2016, two young Palestinian men, Ramzi al-Qasrawi and Abdul Fattah al-Sharif, were murdered by Israeli soldier, Elor Azaria. Your husband Imad famously filmed the moment when Azaria shot al-Sharif in the head. Can you tell us about that day?

That day, the children went to school, and workers came to renovate the house. I made them coffee, but we couldn't drink it because we heard shooting. I went outside very quickly. There was a Palestinian worker on our roof and he said that the soldiers had shot somebody. Imad went out with bare feet. I carried the camera and went out after my husband. My husband shouted, "they shot him!" I gave him the camera. The man was lying on the ground and moving a little bit. I was saying, "he's alive." A mother's feeling is very strong. I started shouting at the soldiers, "he's my brother, he's my neighbour." This attracted the attention of the soldiers, so I told Imad to film elsewhere. The soldiers pulled me out from behind the wall and two soldiers held onto each of my hands. I noticed that my husband was on our neighbour's roof, and he shook his head, indicating to me not to tell the soldiers where he was.

When Imad was on the neighbour's roof, one of the soldiers moved the body of the victim with his foot. I said, "you should be merciful, he is still alive." The soldiers said, "he is a terrorist." The soldier was saying that he had a suicide belt on and I said, "no, let me approach him." Imad filmed from the roof and revealed the crime. May God be merciful on the victim.

It was a Jewish holiday – Purim – and the soldiers brought water tanks over and washed the blood [from the street]. Annette Cohen [a notoriously violent religious settler] was giving sweets to the soldiers [to celebrate the killing]. There is footage of [the murderer], Azaria, shaking hands with Baruch Marzel [a local Israeli settler and right-wing extremist politician] and Ofer [the medic who moved the knife closer to the body].*

Baruch Marzel leads a settler movement and was a close friend and colleague of Baruch Goldstein who committed the massacre in the Ibrahimi Mosque, killing 15 Palestinians during Ramadan in 1994. Ofer is an infamous settler paramedic [whose violence has been exposed by Palestinians] and [he has been] banished from his work as a result.

[After the shooting] Imad was shocked. It was hard for him to believe that he had filmed the death. We started having lots of phone calls. My phone was ringing constantly, with people wanting to know about the incident. It spread very quickly.

For a month I was afraid. I had seen them executing him. I was worried about my family, and told my husband that we should live somewhere else. My husband received death threats and

*In 2021, Ofer – the same Israeli colonist mentioned in this interview – shot a Palestinian woman dead in Hebron. Her name was Wafa' Abdul-Rahim Barade'ey. Independent Middle East Media Center wrote at the time: "An Israeli military spokesperson tried to claim that the Palestinian woman was armed and had opened fire with an M-16 rifle, and some Israeli media outlets took the narrative for granted and even reported the incident was an attempted stabbing attack, pictures from the scene show the woman posed no threat to the soldiers, or anybody else. What they show is an armed paramilitary settler taking a knee to aim before killing her. The gun he used is then seen planted near her body, as if she had been the one holding it."

we were threatened with being burnt.

After the murder, the Israeli soldiers closed the area more tightly. Until now we are denied visitors [under military order]. At the end of Ramadan, the family usually visits each other in our homes, but this year my family cannot visit anyone.

For two years [after 2015], we were treated like numbers. Israeli soldiers issued us special IDs with numbers allocated to each Palestinian who lives in the neighbourhood. We would be called by numbers, not names, as if we were not humans. At checkpoints, soldiers would say for example, "number 20 is allowed, but number 66 (my number) is not allowed".

It was horrible, and every time they changed the Israeli Forces operating in the area, they would change our numbers. If our numbers weren't detected at checkpoint, because of a technical error they made, they would turn our lives into hell.

Can you talk more about the psychological impact of life under occupation, especially for women and children?

Our suffering is endless under the occupation. During a night raid they confiscated my kitchen knives. Now I have to smuggle in small knives for peeling oranges.

Our children become irritated. When will children have their freedom to play here? Our children play in the street and don't have a playground, and the soldiers grab their footballs and destroy them. Palestinian children all go and buy toy guns. It's forbidden [by the occupation] for our children to fly kites. The children have bikes and they want to take them out, but the soldiers won't open the side gate of the checkpoint [to let them through].

The army sometimes [confiscates] the kids' bikes. I once videoed soldiers taking the ball of a child and putting it inside their checkpoint.

Children can't carry compasses to school because they're banned by the Israelis. They have to keep them at school. I want to launch a campaign for the children, to talk about their rights and their suffering. I want to give them toys to play with in the streets. It's a basic right for children. Where should the children go to play here? There is a community centre in the south part of the city with a swimming pool, but we need to pass at least three checkpoints to go to that place.

I am worried all the time. Every time I pass these checkpoints I risk my life. But I don't want to restrict myself and I don't want my girls to be shy. I don't want them to be stuck in the house. I want them to have pride and the will for freedom. I want them to believe that we will achieve that. I want them to be brave. But I have less control over my boys. My son, Saleh, is fond of videoing. He's holding the camera all the time. And at least half of the soldiers know his name.

One high school girl was on her period and had sanitary pads in her bag. The soldiers wanted to force her to put everything on the table [at a checkpoint]. This is very sensitive in our culture. Now, every time she is on her period she won't go to school. Her mother explained it to the school, and the principle put sanitary towels in school.

The women avoid wearing belts, because we are asked to take them off at checkpoints. We don't want to be asked to strip or take off part of our clothes, and there's no female soldiers in our particular checkpoint. Sometimes women buy underwear and then soldiers ask us to open our bags. It's embarrassing. Sometimes the bottom of our shoes are metal so the metal detectors go off.

Sometimes they ask us to take off our headscarves or jackets. One girl had a short-sleeved T-shirt beneath her jacket. The soldier insisted that she took off her coat. The girl didn't want to, and the soldier said to her, "you are hiding a knife."A Palestinian man was there, and he said to the soldier, "I won't leave because you might kill the girl." I came and helped her to take off the jacket. We had to make a bad choice to prevent the worst. Afterwards, that girl started going round the back way through the olive groves to avoid the checkpoints.

Sometimes we have specific cases of women having cancers and living in the area. But Palestinian ambulances can't get to our neighbourhood. Six families left our neighbourhood because no-one would ask their daughters to marry them, as people can't get access to go into our area. Even the young men in our neighbourhood get refused because they don't want their daughters to come and live in this area. Most of the youths who are from the neighbourhood go and live somewhere else. Palestinian society grows fast but in Tel Rumeida the population remains the same because young men and women get married and leave.

Do you have any final thoughts you'd like to share?

I'd like [international] solidarity groups to support Palestinian women who live close to the settlers, to give women opportunities for projects in their homes, because women have to stay in their houses to protect them [from settlers].

The best form of solidarity is to support our existence on our lands, which is getting more difficult day by day. Tel Rumeida used to be a home for thousands of families, but due to the realities of settler violence and military closure, we are now just 130 families, all fighting a daily struggle for survival and existence. It is a moral and political responsibility for all of us not to let Israeli settler movements win, and to maintain Palestinian existence. We have a lot of creativity and ideas that could support our shrinking community but we lack the means.

So, many families live off the olive harvest season. But even that is under threat because Israeli settlers' attacks escalate during this season. They hope to drive us out of our home through attacking our means of living and economy. Some of the olive fields we have here go back to the Roman times and we ache when we see the trees being attacked as part of the Zionist reprisal techniques against us. If we have enough support we can coordinate for members of our community to protect these harvests and deploy its production for maintaining our existence on the land.

All women have their suffering. Every time our tears dry we get more tears. But despite all the difficulties we continue smiling. I hope that I am succeeding in showing the voice of Palestinian society from a woman's perspective because it is always the men who talk about this. Now my camera is my weapon.

Amal Awad
Ramallah, West Bank

We interviewed Amal (a pseudonym) in a cafe in Ramallah about being a queer woman in the West Bank and about LGBTQIA+ organising in Palestine. Amal is involved with Al Qaws, A grassroots Palestinian movement for sexual & gender diversity in Palestinian society.

What does it mean to be queer in Palestine?

In Al Qaws we use the term queer because it doesn't only imply a sexual identity; it also implies a political identity.

Most queer people I know are undercover, living a double life. Some decide to get married to someone that they don't love just to please their parents. It's taboo to talk about being queer.

Even for queers themselves it takes them time to accept themselves. Even me, when I was young I was told it was a sickness and that it was disgusting. Everyone told me this: that's the idea people have of homosexual people here. Sometimes it's easier to keep it quiet and try and change yourself, just to please everyone else. People can get kicked out of the family house and the village [for being queer]. So instead people say to themselves "even if I'm unhappy, I'm safe".

It's not [only] challenging like this for LGBT people, it's also difficult for unmarried couples and anyone else who chooses to live a different lifestyle and to make different decisions.

Is the situation changing at all in the West Bank?

For queer people it's very challenging, but it's changing a little bit. Al Qaws is doing work with schools, lawyers and journalists and you can now even hear about their work on the radio. Al Qaws has a hotline you can call for support. There are workshops organised sometimes in Ramallah. We have groups in Jerusalem, Jaffa, Haifa and Ramallah that you can join. This wouldn't have been possible five years ago. Al Qaws has been working for fifteen years in Palestine but only for [four] years officially in the West Bank.

From my observation - at least in Ramallah - younger queer people are [becoming] more comfortable with how they dress and behave. I'm not saying that you can be open, but I'm seeing that more young people are more relaxed about it.

Al Qaws tries to make it possible for queers to live in Palestine, and avoid them seeking safety where there is none, like in Tel Aviv for example. Al Qaws believes that you cannot separate the political context from the personal identities and thus we are actively raising awareness internationally and locally against 'pink-washing'.* We as Palestinians believe that if we

---

*'Pink-washing' refers to the portrayal of the state of Israel as a progressive queer-friendly place, covering up the colonial violence faced by queer Palestinians. In fact, the image of Israel as a place that is tolerant to queer people is blatantly untrue. The annual Pride march in Tel Aviv has been the subject of repeated violent attacks, including stabbings, by members of Israel's Orthodox Jewish community.

want a free country, then we have to free ourselves as well – women, gays, people with special needs, people with different skin colours. An inclusive liberation movement.

I have heard many different stories of people being arrested by the Palestinian Authority. There aren't any laws that say 'if you're gay you go to prison', but people still get arrested without charge. Many people have difficult times and struggle living their daily lives.

Is there resistance to Al Qaws' organising in the West Bank?

Yes, Al Qaws has encountered resistance. It's not easy. For example, the trainers do workshops and trainings with therapists to take into consideration the special context of being gay in Palestine. Al Qaws trains the social workers in schools - and anyone who is interested in taking this training - so that they actually support and help people. We also did a training for a Palestinian human rights organisation.

Doing meetings and lectures means that our organising is visible, but we try to be careful because we want to protect our members and activists. Many people who come to Al Qaws don't want to be visible. They have to be careful. If we [decide] to be visible, it's because we want to have an impact on therapists, schools, universities: those who have direct contact with queer people.

Being queer is also a type of activism. Being who you are, getting out of the system. We can't forget that if you're not [accepted for] who you are then it also creates a lot of social problems. How would a [queer] woman – or man – feel about sleeping with [someone] that she has no emotions towards? By forcing people to be who they aren't, you're oppressing people and that brings a lot of problems. There shouldn't be so much resistance to diversity in our society. As long as I'm not hurting you and I'm just wanting to live my life, I'm not [negatively] affecting society as a whole and I can be very productive. Being queer doesn't change the fact that you can be a good, happy, healthy, productive person. Why not have a society that is diverse, where people accept each other? Why can't we see it as a value? It's a blessing to have such a diverse range of people.

We think that queer people living in Palestine have their own specific needs. Most of the time the West puts queers in the Middle East all in the same box. But you can't just put people in the same category because they speak the same language.

Can you talk a bit more about Israel's pink-washing and 'normalisation'* programmes?

We refuse the idea that Israel is a safe haven for Palestinian gays, because it's not true. They're still oppressing us and they're still a big part of our daily challenges. Pink-washing is a way to turn the attention away from Israel being the occupier and instead talk about Israel as this really gay-friendly state. That's very problematic. I don't think a Palestinian who had just moved to Tel Aviv would feel safe or would feel that it's a

*'Normalisation' refers to the normalisation of relations with the Israeli occupation of Palestine. The word is often used to refer to the normalisation of relations between Israel and Arab or Muslim states. This state level normalisation is promoted by the US, with states that sign agreements with Israel being rewarded by US funding. This process has happened with states such as Egypt, Jordan or, most recently, UAE. However 'normalisation' also refers to civil society initiatives which try to promote an unequal cooperation between Israelis and Palestinians.

place where they have everything they need. What we try to do is educate people that if they go to Pride in Tel Aviv they're participating in the colonial system and its ideology.

Initiatives like Seeds of Peace* are also part of normalisation processes. I can't talk about peace if I can still see the occupation. If we have freedom and equality then I can talk about peace. But I can't talk about it if I go through this every day. So I don't collaborate with queer people in Israel.

Even left-wing Israelis, what are they doing? Are they paying their taxes to Israel, are they going to the army? If you say you're a left-wing Israeli but you do this then you're being hypocritical.

What do West Bank schools teach about sexuality?

In schools here there is no mention of queer politics. We have sex education at a very late age. Even for queer people it's hard to accept themselves because the things that you know are the things you learn from society and the internet.

In general, do you think there's a lot of pressure from within the family to marry?

Yes. For women the pressure always starts earlier than men. It depends on your family. But I would say it starts at 24 years old for women and 30 for men. Then the nagging starts: "when are we going to see you with children?" Family pressure, friends

---

*Seeds of Peace is a US-based NGO that organises camps for Palestinians, Israelis and people from other Arab countries aimed at 'leadership development'. Their website includes posts about queer issues.

pressure, social pressure. There's also pressure for people who want to get divorced, especially women. People look at you as if your life has ended if you want to get divorced, and always say it's the fault of the woman.

What is it like for trans people in the West Bank?

It's a big, big taboo. Also we don't have the clinics and hospitals that would give you a transition. Palestinians have to transition in Israel. I know people who consider themselves trans but they didn't go through the transition. But at the parties that Al Qaws organises they find the space to be who they want to be. It's one of the toughest situations. Because you're not only saying you have a different sexual preference. [In the eyes of mainstream society] you're saying that you're refusing 'the body that God gave you'.

Is there anything else you would like to share with us?

We don't like to be looked at as poor Palestinian women who have no rights and who are being oppressed by their men. We don't like to be pitied. We still feel like we're blessed to be here. People are still very happy with what they have. It's important to know that there is a daily struggle to stay here [in Palestine]. Even just to be here and live your normal life is a kind of resistance. But at the same time we love it here. Maybe people see us as being imprisoned here, but we still love it despite all the difficulties and the challenges, and that gives us a reason to wake up every day.

Rana Abu Rahmah
Bil'in, West Bank

We interviewed Rana at the house where she lives with her husband in the village of Bil'in in 2018. Rana is a journalist and filmmaker, who has been involved in the popular struggle against the Israeli occupation. We interviewed her on a Friday, and as we spoke the family were watching live footage of the Great March for Return protests in Gaza. The footage showed Israeli forces shooting tear gas and live ammunition at Palestinian demonstrators, and injured people being carried away on stretchers.

Could you tell us a bit about your background?

I moved to Bil'in when I married my husband Ashraf. I'm originally from Nablus, and I used to live in a camp called Camp Number One, because it was the first camp established [in Nablus].*

I first became an activist, and then a journalist. But I didn't

*According to the United Nations Reliefs Works Agency (UNWRA): "Camp No. 1 was established in 1950 and borders the Nablus municipality. It was the first camp established in the Nablus area and was thus named Camp No. 1. It is also known as Ein Beit el-Ma'. Israeli army incursions into the camp are not uncommon and frequently result in arrests, as well as damage to homes." With nearly 7,500 registered persons in the camp, Camp No. 1 is the West Bank's most densely populated camp.

study journalism – I studied business management.

After I finished high school I worked on a local TV channel called *Al-Afaq* – which means 'horizons' – but it was shut down by the Israeli army in 2015. At *Al-Afaq* we covered breaking news and we followed everything up 24/7, so the army felt that this threatened them and their plans. They came and invaded the building, which was in Area A [the area of the West Bank which was designated as under Palestinian control during the Oslo Agreements in the early 1990s] and sealed it off.

I was also in a campaign called *We Refuse To Die Silently*, based in a few places in the West Bank. I was the only woman in the campaign, except for Nariman Tamimi [a woman involved in the popular resistance from the village of Nabi Saleh]. We would have four people in a car – a driver, a [Palestinian] volunteer, an international volunteer and a Palestinian journalist – and go to the villages located close to settlements to help people to gather olives from their farms [as Palestinian farmers are routinely harassed by the settlers and army when picking their olives].

The camera can somehow protect people from the soldiers. We documented a lot of things that the soldiers and the settlers did. The international volunteers were from ISM [the International Solidarity Movement].

Were you treated with respect by the men in the campaign?

No, it wasn't easy. The men had this thing about thinking they were stronger, even though I did the same job as them. When settlers or soldiers came, the men would say to be careful and try to keep me back. But during those moments I didn't think about if I was a man or a woman: I was just thinking that something should be done.

Every Friday we used to go to [the village of] Kufr Qadum — which is close to Nablus — to be with the local people and film [the protests]. On the first anniversary of [the] Kufr Qadum [protests], I made a film about the village and gave it to the people. I kept on going there for about two years.

How did the men react to you in Kufr Qadum?

When I first went there they asked me why I was there. "There are enough people here," they said, "so why a woman?" Sometimes I felt that this view existed in how people looked at me, even if they didn't say anything. My counter-argument whenever we had this discussion was: "I'm standing next to an international woman [activist] and I'm doing exactly what she does, so why should I stay at home?" Then we started to ask, why don't the women of the village participate? So we became involved in talking with women. For example, I saw an old woman who was participating in activities [resisting the occupation] running after a soldier with her shoe.

There was no filming at first in Kufr Qadum, I was the first one to do it. So this [established my reputation] there. I proposed establishing a media unit. So I went and started training [people in media], and I became a trainer for the people who went into the field. Since then a lot of barriers vanished. So it was difficult but not impossible.

Were you scared, being in Kufr Qadum while soldiers were firing at demonstrators?

It's dangerous in Kufr Qadum because there's one street, and on either side is [olive groves] and [there is a big risk that] you will either get shot or arrested. Of course I was scared. I was once hit by a tear gas bomb. I didn't go to hospital, but it has affected my back.

Can you tell us about your work supporting the families of prisoners?

There was a man called Khader Adnan who was on hunger strike in prison for about two months.* Because of that I became more involved in [working with] the families of prisoners. We used to put up [protest] tents so the families of prisoners would gather there. We filmed the protests and other activities and I made a film about it, along with a director. The protests were mainly in city centres like Arafat Square in Ramallah, and sometimes at other places like Ofer prison [a military prison close to Ramallah]. A lot of prisoners' families used to go there.

We started the *Asra Voice – Voice of the Prisoners* – radio network, and from 2012 to 2015 I worked on it. The prisoners' families called the radio station and talked about their sons. The prisoners could also hear the radio in jail. It was a connection between the families of the prisoners and the prisoners themselves. I was one of the people responsible for preparing the day-to-day tasks of the show, and I used to interview the families at the [protest] tents. I'd also go to the prisoners' families' houses and record what they said [for the

*Khader Adnan went on hunger strike for 66 days in 2012, bringing him close to death. He was released as a result of the hunger strike, but has subsequently been arrested several times.

radio show]. We used to choose the families who had special cases: for example, those whose parents were very old and couldn't visit their son, or those who were not allowed to visit their relatives in jail.

There was a program for prisoners and a program for families of martyrs [people who have lost their lives as a result of Israel's occupation]. I started as a volunteer and then they gave me basic expenses to work on the other show about the martyrs.

How do you think the presence of cameras at a demonstration changes things?

The presence of cameras is very important. A good example is when [my husband] Ashraf's own phone was used to film his arrest. [To give another example,] Ashraf's brother Bassem was shot [with a tear gas canister and killed] in 2009.* The camera

*According to the Forensic Architecture website: "On 17 April 2009, near the village of Bil'in, Bassem Abu Rahma was shot and killed by a tear-gas canister fired across the fence of the barrier wall that surrounds the West Bank. Abu Rahma was attending a protest, and was unarmed.

The protest occurred at a location that had been declared a 'closed military zone' by Israeli authorities four years earlier. Since then, non-violent activists were routinely arrested and imprisoned in the area.

In the context of such encounters, official instructions allow soldiers to use only 'non-lethal means', such as tear gas and rubber-coated bullets, unless their lives are in danger. But while tear gas is considered a 'non-lethal' munition, when the aluminum gas canister hits a human body directly, the impact can be fatal. Soldiers are only supposed to shoot these munitions upward, at a trajectory of 60 degrees, above a crowd.

Following Abu Rahma's death, the military denied responsibility, claiming that soldiers did not fire the canister directly at the victim."

was there but the ambulance was not. His sister Jawaher inhaled tear gas mixed with white phosphorus but when she died, there was no camera.*

Rana's husband Ashraf interrupts to explain what happened to his brother:

Bassem was asking the soldiers not to shoot tear gas because there were sheep in the area. So they shot him with a [high velocity] tear gas canister straight into his heart. This canister can travel a kilometre and a half in distance, and the way the soldiers used it is illegal. The soldiers were close to Bassem and the canister opened his chest and went in by about ten centimetres.

Rana continues:

The camera showed the reality of what happened to Bassem. The soldiers said that the canister ricocheted off a post and then into his chest. But the video showed exactly what happened. If there's no camera, the occupation will always refute what actually happened. These videos show the reality of what actually happens. The Israeli army tries to delete videos like this. All of a sudden you see that videos like this disappear.

*An Independent Middle East Media Center news report from January 2011 reads: "Jawaher Abu Rahma, aged 35, died on Saturday, after suffering the effects of tear gas inhalation fired by the Israeli military during the Friday weekly protest in Bil'in. Medical sources reported that the cause of the death was suffocation from tear gas chemicals mixed with phosphorus. Hundreds of Palestinians, internationals and Israeli peace activists attended Abu Rahma's funeral in a procession through the village of Bil'in on Saturday, in which residents released a statement condemning the death."

In October 2017 the soldiers raided our house at 3 am, along with other families in the village. They wanted to talk to Ashraf, but Ashraf wasn't there. I filmed when they came in. My voice was loud because I was stressed. The soldiers told me not to speak. In the video I was saying, "don't touch anything." They were checking everything, and I was filming them. They took all of our devices and technology. During the raid, the soldiers had a scary-looking person with them, who had his face covered and wore gloves. He looked like a technology expert. They must have had something that tracks technology because they went straight to our closet and found a hard disk.

We had lost any hope of getting our devices back, but they returned them after two months. When we got them back, they were broken. They hacked the phone so whatever SIM card you put in, it doesn't work any more.

The Israeli authorities are trying to make it illegal for people to film the army.* What do you think of that?

They don't want their crimes to be documented. This [proposed] law means that whoever takes photos or videos of soldiers will go to jail for five to ten years. But if we stick to every new law imposed by the occupation, we won't be able to leave our houses. We are under occupation and there is no justice under occupation. People won't care about this new law: they will keep filming. Their videos are holy to them – for example, when they want to show evidence in court of people throwing rocks – but filming is a crime for us.

*In 2018 a bill on the "Prohibition against photographing and documenting IDF Soldiers" was presented to the Israeli parliament. The bill aimed to make the photographing of soldiers punishable by 10 years in prison.

They came up with this law because Imad Abu Shamsiyah filmed the murder of a young man, shot [by an Israeli soldier] in Hebron. So nowadays the cameras scare them. They have recently shot journalists [for example on the Great March of Return protests in Gaza].* If they don't shoot them, they arrest them. The camera is the first line of defence.

In Gaza, on the Great March of Return, they have been targeting journalists...

They are targeting the elements that are saving people's lives. Of course they target journalists, especially when Palestine became a member of the UN and Israel felt that the PA would somehow sue them under international law, so they felt that [the evidence gathered by journalists affected them]. Now Palestine will sue Israel under international law because of [evidence provided by] the cameras – we have the evidence and the Palestinian narrative is winning over the Israeli one.

Are you still doing videography?

After moving to Bil'in I stopped doing video journalism. There are a lot of journalists in Bil'in and it's a small village!

Are there any organisations for female journalists in Palestine?

No. There's no possibilities for such a thing. [Equipment is also a problem]. I have been to a lot of demonstrations but I'm never

---

*For example, soldiers shot and killed Yaser Murtaja during the Great March of Return protests. He was wearing a jacket emblazoned with the word 'Press'.

wearing a bullet-proof vest. I don't have one because they're very expensive and there's no-one to give it to me.

Do you think it is more difficult for a woman to get involved in political organising in the West Bank than it is for a man?

Yes, its not easy, because our society is conservative. In terms of filming, I felt that the camera gave me strength. It felt like a person supporting me. And when I became involved with the prisoners and their families, I acted out of empathy because [one day] I might be the one who needs support when someone I love goes to jail.

Ghada Hamdan
Om Sleiman farm, Bil'in

We met with Ghada (a pseudonym) in Jerusalem in the summer of 2018. We spoke to her about permaculture and cooperatives in the West Bank.

Ghada is part of Om Sleiman, a permaculture farm which has been established in the village of Bil'in. Om Sleiman is situated on a piece of land which has been the subject of years of struggle. It lies close to the Israeli colony of Modi'in Illit.

In 2005 the Israeli apartheid wall began to be built in Bil'in, and the land where Om Sleiman now lies was annexed by Israel. A struggle began, with local Palestinians waging popular demonstrations against the wall. In the ensuing Israeli repression many villagers were imprisoned, or lost their lives. The village's struggle has become famous worldwide.

In 2010, as a result of years of direct action, the people managed to claim back 30% of the annexed land – including the land of Om Sleiman – and the wall was re-routed.

The farm is still, however, based in 'Area C', meaning that the land is under full Israeli control and the Palestinian farmers of Om Sleiman are forbidden from building any structures, including wells. The existence of the farm is an act of resistance in itself.

Why did you choose to be involved in land-based organising?

I choose farming as a form of activism and resistance, especially permaculture, because it shows how you can make solutions out of problems. It gives you tools to get over them.

I'm really interested in self-sufficiency because that's what's really missing in Palestine. Palestinians are dependent on the Israeli occupation for food and water. Israel controls everything; we don't even have an independent economy of our own. And this is really dangerous and risky. We have to learn to be independent, self-sufficient, to harvest our own water and build our own homes.

There was a big movement aimed at building self-sufficiency and autonomy during the First Intifada. Has the situation changed now?

The structures of our neighbourhoods in the First Intifada were different. Back then people lived in small communities and everyone knew each other and would know what their neighbours' professions were. You had the farmer, the cheese maker, the people who did maintenance. People needed each other. Now everything is available everywhere and you don't need your friends. People don't know their neighbours and this has created a big gap, a bit like in western society: individualistic. This is especially the case in Ramallah and in Jerusalem. The young people running away from the villages are fed up with people knowing everything about their lives so they're tending to go for the individualist approach.

Are cooperatives politically significant for you?

Definitely. I believe in co-ops. You share the [economic] risk and you have a group to lean on and support you. But it has to be done very carefully, because it can be destructive sometimes. [For example,] we don't need cooperatives growing food using chemicals.

The villages used to be a good [cooperative] system; for example, a villager would have a field of corn and people would help [to harvest] and share the food. There was a more voluntary way of living. Now people don't know the meaning of voluntarism.

How strong are ecological movements in Palestine?

Ecological ideas are becoming more popular. But I don't know whether that's just because it's a trend in the world. I don't know if its just the hipster style, or because people are really sick of the NGOs, the PA [Palestinian Authority] and the occupier and they want an alternative way of living. But it's definitely growing, especially amongst the youngsters.

But it's still not big enough, and it doesn't go beyond buying organic food. Not many people are going back to the villages and farming. People are always thinking about the obstacles, [for example,] that they don't have the skills, or the land is too expensive.

The system has created a comfortable bubble. It's created a situation where it's difficult to imagine an alternative way of living. A system that makes you want to stay inside it, even if you hate it. You are in the office 8 am til 4 pm, and go out at the weekend, and repeat. One of the hardest things is to get out of your comfort zone and head towards an alternative way of life.

If you're producing your own food, that's already alternative. If you quit your job, that's an alternative. If you make your own vinegar, oil or cheese, that's an alternative. If you build your house from mud [a traditional Palestinian building style], that's an alternative.

The language we speak has to be different. We take language for granted. But I think language is an important tool to attract people to participate in something bigger.

In the last few years NGOs have really spread here in Palestine and have brought their own language. Words like 'development' and 'strategic'. They're using language brought from the outside and the language is also occupying us and taking us away from our own language and vocabulary. Even people who don't speak English know what these NGO words mean.

Can you explain your critique about the word 'development'?

I don't like the word 'development' because it makes me feel that the Third World countries are poor, ignorant and backwards, that we need to work to catch up with the 'developed' countries.

They call us undeveloped countries. But we have a different way of living and culture, and they're trying to make us jump 100 years. The way they talk about gender, violence, poverty, women. People coming with building projects and putting a sign up saying 'US AID': that's not developing. It's the opposite. But the funders won't fund a project if they can't put up their sign and their flag.

Can you talk more about the effect of Western NGOs on Palestinian society, and on farmers?

Working for an NGO is considered to be a good middle class job. But if these NGOs are dependent on Western funds, your project starts to depend on the agendas of Western NGOs, as it's them that make the decisions about what they will fund. They will make you sign papers about who you can collaborate with. They say that you can't collaborate with terrorists: people they define as Hamas, someone who was in prison, someone who threw rocks at the Israeli army. A terrorist for them could be a freedom fighter for us.

There's a school called Dalal Mughrabi, named after a woman resistance fighter who was part of Fatah.* She was born in [Sabra] refugee camp [in Beirut]. She participated in an attack and she died here [in Palestine].** For Palestinians she's a hero. For internationals she's a terrorist. One [funder] said that they wanted the name of the school to change, or they would stop funding it.

The NGOs impact society in a very negative way. For example, if a Palestinian NGO wants to do a project, then they're thinking with the heads of foreigners. They do a project and, whenever

*Fatah is formally known as the Palestinian National Liberation Movement. Established in 1967, Fatah engaged in armed struggle aimed at national liberation. Fatah now controls the Palestinian Authority.

**Dalal Mughrabi and a group of Fatah fighters landed near Tel Aviv in 1978 and hijacked a bus. She was killed in a shootout with Israeli forces. In 2013, the Belgian government suspended funding for two school construction projects in the Palestinian territories after it emerged that a school it had funded was named Mughrabi.

they leave, people are back to zero because the projects aren't sustainable.

US AID [the United States Agency for International Development] did this with Palestinian farmers. They came with a new kind of cucumber. The small ones. They said,"here's the seeds, you don't have to pay anything". The farmers tried it for the first season. The next year they said that "you have to pay for the spray". The following year they said that "you have to pay for everything yourselves". By this time the farmers were in so much debt, and the soil was dead. When everyone plants the same crops, that means they won't be able to sell it. In some cases [these US AID projects] been done in collaboration with the Palestinian Ministry of Agriculture.

A similar thing happened [when Israel occupied the West Bank] in 1967. Israel announced that all the resources of this land belong to the [Israeli] state, and they went to the Palestinian farmers and gave them seeds and chemicals and told them how to plant things. That's a way to control food, and also to gain control of our knowledge. [Back then] Palestinians were producing 80% of our needs and we were exporting sesame. Now we're importing everything from Israel and abroad. What the Palestinian Authority spends on agriculture is maybe 4% of the GDP – it's nothing. Even our most traditional foods like sesame are imported now.

What is your position on accepting funding at Om Sleiman?

"The farm started with a no-fund policy for the first three years, following that we decided to accept [grants] from local organisations, [as long as they were unconditional], to fund projects and education programs. I think that when it comes to funds it's not white or black. The owner of the land gave us the land for free: isn't it some sort of funding? When we had an accident at the farm and lost all our seed stock and we were able to recover our costs in a week because the community helped us right away, isn't it a sort of community fund? We see the importance of having the production side of the farm as self-sufficient, meaning the membership fees paid by our customers for the price of the vegetables should cover the cost of producing these crops. But [if we did] other projects we could have a great effect on our nature and society. Why say no to individuals who want to donate to a project they feel proud of?

There's now more small farms [like Om Sleiman] and we try to share our skills because the others aren't organic or natural. They come and ask questions and see the results of our work. Maybe they will consider it when they go back to their farms.

What is your financial model at Om Sleiman?

We are a community-supported agriculture farm, meaning that people sign up for the whole season usually – three months' pay in advance – in exchange for a weekly basket of our fresh organic produce. There is a direct relationship between consumers and us. We don't have to worry about marketing our produce, or getting money before we start the season.

What members pay for is how much it costs us to grow. It might not be affordable for some people but we offer discounts and you can come volunteer in exchange for products as well.

What do you think of the international Boycott Divestment and Sanctions (BDS) movement?

I support the boycott movement, especially to influence the people abroad. Israel wants international support and to be able to do business abroad. If Israel feels excluded and alone, and no-one wants to do business with them, then they will start reconsidering what they're doing. I support BDS but it shouldn't be the only way we resist.

We need to struggle in other ways too. For example, natural farming, education, art, culture, fighting back [by throwing] rocks. I believe that each person chooses their own way of resistance.

Palestinians have been so patient. We're too hospitable with the occupation. I think definitely the first step should be that people learn to change society from the inside. They don't know where their food is coming from. They go to the supermarket and they don't realise that it's the garbage of Israel being sold to them.

What do you think about the factory farming of animals in Palestine?

Traditionally, people in Palestinian villages kept animals. But I don't think people are aware [of the realities] of factory farms: they imagine chickens running around freely. And it's not like people visit the farm and see the thousands of chickens on top of each other. I don't think people make a connection between what they eat and the creature. When they order chicken it's just meat. They don't think about the living creature who had a life span.

Do you think people in Palestine have a strong connection to the land?

Since we were young we're told through music and art how beautiful Palestine is. But I think some of these things were forced upon us. Those who are refugees, if you ask them how they imagine Palestine they will say, olive trees, so beautiful, so clean, so green. But I don't think that's true in our actions sometimes. It's hard to get rid of tradition, religion, flags, politics.

I think the older generation, who worked on the land every day, know how precious it is and how much it can give you. Later generations never worked on the land, and they don't know how important it is. I don't think you can love your land if you're neglecting it or using chemicals on it.

[Some people are trying to preserve the Palestinian natural heritage], such as Vivien Sansour,* who has a seed library and is very active in saving seeds and giving them to farmers.

The younger generation has other interests. There is a big gap in society: between people trying to come back to their land and culture and those who are attracted by other things. Some people are really hypnotised by consumerism… these people are zombies. They don't stop and think about what they're

---

*Vivien Sansour is the founder of the Palestine Heirloom Seed Library. Her website states: "The Palestine Heirloom Seed Library (PHSL) is an attempt to recover these ancient seeds and their stories and put them back into people's hands. The PHSL is an interactive art and agriculture project that aims to provide a conversation for people to exchange seeds and knowledge, and to tell the stories of food and agriculture that may have been buried away and waiting to sprout like a seed. It is also a place where visitors may feel inspired by the seed as a subversive rebel, of and for the people, travelling across borders and checkpoints to defy the violence of the landscape while reclaiming life and presence."

doing. Even if [we didn't have] capitalism, it would be a really shitty alternative.

[There is a culture here that] even if you have no idea about what you want to learn, you go to university, graduate, get a masters, get married, have children with a husband that you have never lived with before. Most of the time you're told what to do by your parents, teachers, bosses. It's really hard to get out of this prison. I think it's applicable all over the world. It's really hard to get out of traditions, and you have to please everyone all the time. I know many people who are living a life that they have never chosen because they want to please people, or because they were too scared to try anything different.

Can you tell us about feminism in Palestine?

Here we have feminist women who don't even know they're feminist. West of Ramallah there's 900 dunums* of land controlled by women. It's all run by women. They plant, they weed, they seed, they harvest. For me this is feminist. All the men go to work in the settlements and the women have to be responsible for covering the needs of their families. That's feminism, but [these women] don't know what feminism is.

Women have always been part of the Palestinian resistance. Many freedom fighters are women. That's also feminism. The term feminism can be problematic if you try to apply the approach of the West with [our] situations, that [doesn't] work

---

*A dunum, also known as a donum or dunam, was the Ottoman unit of land equivalent to the English acre, representing the amount of land that could be ploughed by a team of oxen in a day.

here. We're still a traditional tribal society. It's problematic if you try to apply it in exactly the same way as in the West. There's NGOs that do that, especially when they come and talk about violence against women with their own terms and language, their own statistics also. The NGOs bring their own language when they talk about women too, it has become so systematic. We're being seen as numbers and not as human beings who have different needs and different lifestyles. The gender roles are sensitive here and you can't create a system based on what's working abroad.

You can support Om Sleiman farm by donating through this link: gofundme.com/f/support-om-sleiman-farm-csa-in-palestine and by sharing the campaign with your friends.

Mona Al-Farra
Gaza

We spoke to Mona Al-Farra over a video call in 2021. Mona is a doctor from Gaza who has spent her life working in grassroots health organisations. We had to stop and start the call several times because of the constant power cuts affecting the Gaza Strip. Mona was recovering from Covid-19 at the time of our interview.

Where were you born and where did your family come from?

I was born in Khan Younis, which is a small town in the southern part of the Gaza Strip, and I lived all my life there until the age of 17, when I went to Cairo to get my first degree in medicine.

Were your family political?

Yes they were. My father was an elected member of the first Palestinian Legislative Council, and he participated in the resistance against the Zionist gangs in Palestine in 1948. I was first politicised by my family background and also the [Israeli] occupation of Palestine in 1967.

When did you become politically active?

I was 13 [in 1967] when Israel occupied Gaza [as well as the

West Bank, East Jerusalem, the Syrian Golan and the Sinai]. The first month [after the occupation] there was resistance. I was in school at the time. I was part of the different demonstrations that took place at that time against the occupation, despite my limited capacity as a young student. With my peers, we did little things like distributing leaflets. At that time there were no printers - they were not allowed by the occupation - so we took on small missions like copying the leaflets and making sure they were distributed.

So this is what we did, and this was going on throughout the Gaza Strip. Some of my colleagues who were a bit older – like 17 or 18 – took part in the resistance as well by helping the freedom fighters in Gaza. Some of them were arrested. But we continued.

After that I went to Cairo to finish my studies, and I returned back after finishing my primary and secondary degrees. When I returned to Gaza, I joined the Union of Health Work Committees (UHWC). Since that time I'm very proud to say that I have always tried to be active within the community and within the UHWC.

How would you describe your politics now?

I vote left... I am a community activist addressing women and children's rights, via different grassroots works. Empowering the community and supporting my people's steadfastness on the ground is my main goal, because I realise that the occupation's long-term strategy is [to bring about] another ethnic cleansing by making life unbearable for Palestinian people in our land.

Can you tell us about the political significance of your medical work?

UHWC is a grassroots health organisation. It was founded by a group of activists [who are] doctors, nurses, pharmacists etc. [When we began] we worked in the refugee camps and in the different parts of the Gaza Strip. At that time there was continuous confrontation between the people in Gaza and the Israeli occupation army. Part of our role [as UHWC] was to serve those who were injured and their families. Besides [that we aimed to] serve the whole community, and our vision was to create medical infrastructure for a future Palestine, because we always thought that we were on the path toward freedom, self-determination and getting our rights. Health must be [considered] amongst all this, and of course most of us are 'left' people so our main vision is to fight privatisation of medicine and to make health services available for the people who need it, especially those who cannot afford even very small fees.

[Through working with UHWC] I had the privilege and honour to be part of a very radical group of men and women, and with them I co-founded a hospital in Jabalia called Al Awda hospital in 1993. 'Al Alwda' in English means 'return', because we as Palestinian people believe that the cornerstone of the Palestinian issue is of course the refugees. What happened in Palestine in 1948, uprooting our people and destroying our villages, [it was] a major ethnic cleansing process that made [hundreds of thousands of] Palestinian people homeless. They were replaced by Israeli Zionists and that's why we strongly believe that the right of return [for Palestinian refugees] is the main issue for us – as part of the process of self-determination and achieving our rights.

So our mission as doctors and health workers, it was not just about providing resources. We also had the vision that we were against privatisation and we were part of the political process in the region. [We were part of this] within our vision, which is mainly a socialist vision.

After we founded Al Awda hospital, I had the idea of setting up health centres and centres for children. The aim of that was to promote health education – in the health centres – and to encourage children with reading and doing different activities like dancing, to keep the Palestinian culture and identity alive. We now have five centres, but in the beginning I founded only two. One [such] centre was in Jabalia refugee camp. Shahd [Abusalama, who was also interviewed for this book], her cousins, her brothers and sisters were part of it. [The centres were about] more than healing, it was about a message of solidarity with the people, with the refugees, with the political prisoners' families, and the families of people who lost their lives while fighting the occupation.

[Later] we set up another centre in Rafah, named after Rachel Corrie.* [One of the purposes of the centre is to be a] platform to connect people [internationally, who want to be] in solidarity with Palestine, with our children.

I also [played] an important part in health education for women. I started a programme called *Women Empowerment Through Health Education.*

*Rachel Corrie was an American volunteer with the International Solidarity Movement. Rachel was crushed to death by an Israeli bulldozer while attempting to stop the demolition of a Palestinian home in Rafah in 2003. She has become an icon of international solidarity amongst Palestinians.

[All of these projects I've mentioned are about] community empowerment. My goal is still the same, supporting people's steadfastness on the ground. I feel this is part of my resistance against the occupation, because the occupation tries – by its different practices – to dehumanise us. Tries to make the environment very bad for our people, to encourage them to leave the country.

I always believe, and still believe, that our existence is resistance. That's why our people are entitled to have somebody, some organisations to help them stay on the ground and to see their needs: health, cultural, social, education etc. This is my means of resistance, this is how I resist the occupation.

I cannot carry a weapon – not because I am weak or a coward – no, because I am older and I am a grandmother now and this is not for me. I believe that resistance is one of our rights according to international law because we are occupied. Wherever you are occupied, you have the right to resist. When, where and how is up to the Palestinian people to decide.

During the Second Intifada the house where you grew up was destroyed by Israeli forces. What was the effect on you?

It had a big impact on me, [and inspired me to continue] my role as a health activist [exposing] the Israeli occupation's brutal acts against the people, like home demolitions, destruction of land, the uprooting of trees, and the killing of civilians during [four] major military attacks and many many air raids.

[These amount to the] continuous violation of human rights,

including health. It goes beyond human rights [violations]. I consider them war crimes.

In 2001 you wrote about the destruction of your family's home in an Israeli feminist magazine called Noga. Do you relate to the word 'feminist'?

In the Palestinian case we all suffer from the occupation, males and females. But the female suffering is doubled due to social and traditional constraints. In that sense I relate to feminism and support its movement.

Have you had a relationship with feminist movements - in Palestine or globally over the years?

Yes I did, with many.

What did your family do after that house was destroyed, where did they go?

My mother was living there, she moved to live with me initially until she sorted out another place.

I continued my life in Gaza and I'm still living in Gaza. I visit the UK to see my children who are living in Manchester and I'm often invited to address communities in Scotland, England and Ireland. I [also] receive many invitations to speak about my people in Australia, America, different countries. I carry a message from thousands of people who are living under the occupation, and explain and educate people about us. Again, this is part of my activism and I believe it is very important because I manage to do a lot of networking with people in solidarity with Palestinian people.

This solidarity is a very important way of resisting the occupation. It helps our people because when I come back from my trips outside Gaza I do another chain of visits telling the people on the ground that they are not alone, they are not forgotten and I tell them about the different activities of different groups in solidarity with the Palestinian people. [I'm] someone who [is able to keep on] moving from Gaza to the outside world - despite the difficulties of the siege, I manage in the end. I believe that through the years the [power of the] solidarity movement has increased in the UK. [It is not the same as] 10 or 20 years ago.

I think this is an important success for all of you who are in solidarity with Palestinian people. I believe the work is continuous because the struggle will continue even after we have got our rights. It is a long way [off], but even after [the end of the occupation] we have another battle which is the struggle of working for social justice in Palestine, and globally as well. So we will continue working. Our activists here [in Gaza] or [outside] should not stop until justice prevails.

During the Israeli attacks in 2006, 2009 and 2014 you were one of the people who communicated a lot with people outside. You wrote a blog – *From Gaza with Love* – about the Israeli attacks. What made you begin to document what was happening? What was it like reporting about the constant attacks on the Palestinians, and did you feel the world was listening?

I started my blog in 2006 but since the Second Intifada, which started at the end of the year 2000, I was continuously writing press releases, exposing the Israeli atrocities against the people. I especially wrote about the abuse of health rights from my position as a physician. So I started writing, writing, writing, sending press releases by email – stories about the children who came to the hospital who were attacked with flechettes [a type of ammunition fired from Israeli aircraft which release thousands of deadly darts]. About the houses that have been evacuated in the middle of the night and about the continuous military incursions into Gaza. Before 2006, there was not a big assault but there were daily atrocities against us.

I always felt that it was my duty to do this, to approach the Western, English-speaking world. And for me it was a way to [express myself] too. I felt good, rather than being worried all the time. Writing gave me the chance to feel that I was putting things on paper with a purpose. It was not just for fun, or a luxury.

After I started my blog I wrote more and more, and as I wrote the atrocities increased as well. Then in 2009 there was a big attack against Gaza.

I was in the UK at that moment, but I travelled quickly to coordinate the medical relief for hospitals in Gaza, including at Al-Awda Hospital. [The attack went on] for 23 days. The attack in 2012 was shorter – like 10 days – but it was very intense, hitting homes and terrorising innocent people. [When Israeli forces] want to target any part of the resistance they don't care who is in the way. Human rights violations were so obvious.

I don't like to call it human rights violations because Israel has exceeded this level. It is war crimes. What is happening in the Occupied Territories, I call it war crimes with confidence. Those people [who are responsible] should be punished for what happened to my people over the years.

After that we had the 2014 attack. I was the deputy chair of the Red Crescent Society for the Gaza Strip, and I was also the head of a Health Committee. I stayed in the health centre for 51 continuous days, interrupted by some ceasefire periods. I coordinated and organised all the health work at that centre. I can say a lot about it but I don't want to put in the details. It was a horror, it was a nightmare and I myself was caught in the fire twice but I escaped being killed. [Israeli forces] targeted hospitals, they targeted schools.

During that time I was working in the health centre until 7 o'clock at night. After that I received many many calls [asking me] to tell the world about what's happening in Gaza. This is very important because I am not a journalist like yourselves, but I am a human being talking from my first-hand experience, so my message was from the heart and from experience. The attack was very under-reported.

I feel sometimes that what we have experienced is not covered well. Right up to this minute we are under daily attack - small attacks. But for the world [to notice] – to talk about us – they need to see [a lot of] bloodshed.

Here in Gaza 2.2 million [of us] are attacked nearly daily, and daily there are attacks on farmers who are just trying to go to their land or the fisherman who are trying to fish. At the moment most of the people in Gaza are in a dire situation.

I'd like to mention something before I forget. And that is that the BDS movement has done very well. I work within the Palestinian NGO Network (PNGO) to encourage people here in Gaza, in hospitals and medical facilities to boycott Israeli companies and we succeeded a great deal. But sometimes we use Israeli products when there is no local alternative [because] we are under occupation.

You have been involved in several movements to break the Israeli blockade from within and without, with international support. How successful do you think these movements have been?

I believe it was very successful. It contributed to more awareness among Western people about our cause, about the occupation and Gaza siege. It was a big act of solidarity, and a chance to expand the solidarity movement. The most important and unique one was the boats to Gaza.

What was your experience during the Great March of Return protests? And how was the international response to the movement?

I was on my way [back to] to Gaza [when the marches began]. I met the Great March of Return members – [who were trying to enter from outside] – in Cairo, and I helped with the [Palestinian NGOs network] statement. [But in the end] the Egyptians did not allow the majority of activists to enter Gaza.

The march members were divided amongst themselves, but I met marvellous comrades in Cairo. We tried to travel via Rafah, but we were not allowed through by the Egyptian authorities. In the end they couldn't enter. I carried eight bags of aid with me to Gaza - medicine mainly - and entered alone after a few tries.

During the Great March of Return, Ahmed Abu Artema – one of the prominent organisers of the March – made public calls for one democratic state in all of historic Palestine,

with equality for Palestinians and Israelis. What do you think of these calls for one democratic state?

This is the future inevitable solution, that will be based on justice and return, as well as long-term prosperity, stability, justice and peace.

It will take time, a very long time, but it will happen as long as there is international will to address peace and justice in Palestine.

What has been your experience during the Covid-19 pandemic?

Our life under occupation has never been, and is still not easy. It is a daily struggle even for the basic things.

Now we are living through the Covid-19 [pandemic]. Civil society organisations have sent many letters explaining how at the moment - and through this pandemic - we are experiencing a new type of apartheid. I call it health apartheid.

In the beginning of the pandemic, no medicine could enter Gaza. Then there was some negotiation and compromise to allow medicine to enter Gaza, [but only] if the resistance here [accepted the constraints put on them by the Israeli military]. It shouldn't be like that, because having accessibility to health and medicine is a basic human right for people according to the Geneva Convention – this is number one. Number two, just a couple of days ago, after big negotiations they did not allow the first 2000 shots [of the Coronavirus vaccine] to enter Gaza. [Now they have allowed the vaccines] to enter Gaza, and in another two weeks we will have another 10,000 shots. [But] compared to the needs of the population this is a very small amount, and always there are obstacles.

When you look at the other side, Israel has managed to give the vaccine to at least 4 million of its population. This is a very high number compared to other Western countries like Britain and the USA. But still they are bargaining with us about [letting in] a few thousand [vaccines] for our population. This is discrimination, war crimes – when you use health for political reasons.

Me, myself, I'm not surprised because we are dealing with an occupying, colonial, racist and apartheid regime. It's a big shame for the world that this so-called 'democracy' is existing in the ruins of other people, who are the original people of the land.

Can you tell us about the work you do now, and its political significance?

I am now the MECA [Middle East Children's Alliance] projects director in Gaza. I design different projects with my team and community-based organisations. [These include projects on] health, water and cultural [projects] – to help keep Palestinian heritage and identity alive. Educational, aid, psychological support via different creative activities. [Building] playing fields for young women and the community, encouraging cycling and other sports.

These activities are politically supporting people's existence on the land, and I also make many links with different political solidarity groups [in my work]. I update them on the current situation, and I convey their message of solidarity from the outside world to Palestine. This [solidarity] message helps my people's psychological well-being, to know that we are not alone and never forgotten.

I am convinced that [this work] is politics, and resistance too.

Are you hopeful about the global political situation and its impact on Gaza?

At the moment, no. But I strongly believe in inevitable world political changes. The Berlin wall collapsed in a day, the Soviet Union too. Apartheid in South Africa is now part of history.

The future will bring up many world changes, and we will never give up our activism and political work toward our different causes, including Palestine.

How hopeful are you about the political situation within Gaza?

I am not hopeful now.

Where does your biggest hope lie when it comes to Palestinian freedom?

With the return [of the refugees] and one democratic state.

What do you think the world that you are struggling for looks like?

Socialism and social justice.

What keeps you going when you feel at your lowest?

Ordinary people in Palestine. Those women, men and children who are struggling daily and never give up under all the difficult circumstances, and endure a great deal of deprivation and injustice.

What would be your advice to younger women who want to make change in Gaza?

Firstly, to believe in themselves as women living under occupation, to believe that they are strong enough to make real change in shaping our future. Secondly, to have clear and focused goals. Thirdly, to work on long-term goals too. Fourthly, to give time to politics and community voluntary work, it has great value in their empowerment, they will realise that later on. And also to learn how it is important to work within a team and to accept differences. To be confident in themselves, to learn more about global struggles. [And lastly] reading, reading and more reading.

What is very important to me as a woman who has spent all my life in this struggle is to pass on the message for younger generations. This is what I am doing now, trying to inspire other people. Because the youth are the future and the work is continuous. This is part of our strength as Palestinians, because we are still on the land. In Gaza [we are] 2.2 million, in the West Bank 3 million, [and we are] keeping the culture and habits.

What they are trying to do in Gaza is a new kind of genocide. Part of that genocide is that they want to destroy our culture our heritage. Me and my comrades, we want to keep the Palestinian identity alive, and not to allow them to crush us with their boots.

Izdihar Afyouni
London, UK

Izdihar is a Palestinian artist and curator living in London. She contributed this article about her experiences in 2021, a year in which the Israeli military launched a full-scale assault on Gaza, and uprisings took place across Palestine. The title of the article is *Inexorable Links*.

This piece of writing has lived through an accelerated carousel of multiple psychological realities of my existence as a diaspora Palestinian artist and activist living as a migrant in England, so please forgive me if it appears to sprout multiple ideological heads in the time it takes you to read. I consider it an informal personal and political recap of 2021 so far; these realities are inexorably linked. For Palestinians, one's personhood is ultimately condemned to be political.

Recently I have been thinking about the ways in which we as Palestinian women can sublimate the degrading and hostile narratives projected onto us by the colonial apparatuses of truth-production, and how to navigate my understanding of myself as an artist and my worth amongst the interpersonal manifestations of that same apparatus as an outspoken migrant woman living in England. After being invited to participate in a group exhibition at a Berlin-based self-professed 'decolonised' art space, I took it upon myself to de-zionize the space itself after they conflated anti-zionism with anti-semitism in a public statement responding to the viral #savesheikhjarrah hashtag in 2021. I have learned that it is not enough to 'take up space' and engage in visibility politics in those art spaces (and by doing so, further facilitate the art-washing of occupation abroad); it is essential to attack, boycott or reform complicit art institutions where possible.

I began working on the third iteration of my project *Thicker Than Blood,* a curatorial biopolitical* analysis of Israel's weaponisation of the coronavirus vaccine in April 2021, three months after Israel declared itself to be the world leader in inoculating its citizens against the coronavirus – and denying five million Palestinians access to the coronavirus vaccine which, as an occupying power, it is obligated to provide under international law. Israeli government officials claimed that the Oslo Accords overruled international law and absolved them of the responsibility to inoculate Palestinians living under occupation. The UN refused this argument and condemned the decision.

Experts at the UN are undoubtedly experts at ultimately useless public condemnations.

The quickly narrowing gap between the political and biological body and its subjection to bio-managing by governments was nothing new for Palestinians living under occupation. Test and

---

*Biopolitics is a concept developed by French philosopher Michel Foucault: "Biopolitics is a complicated concept that has been used and developed in social theory since Michel Foucault, to examine the strategies and mechanisms through which human life processes are managed under regimes of authority over knowledge, power, and the processes of subjectivation." (from https://anthrobiopolitics.wordpress.com/2013/01/21/biopolitics-an-overview/)

trace programmes across the world have illustrated how the government categorises such bodies and how they can then mobilise the divided groups towards vaccination and, eventually, re-entering both working and consumerist spaces. For Palestinians, those who did not hold an Israeli passport would only have access to Israel's supply of the COVID-19 vaccine if they worked for Israeli companies, a decision undertaken by and at the discretion of the Israeli company heads in order to maintain the safety of their Israeli employees.

The geopolitical setting of Israel demands international collaboration with its implementation of medical apartheid against Palestinians living under occupation. This is important to remember when considering Israel's capacity for further political subjectivisation of Palestinian civilians. It has also been one year since Keir Starmer, a self-professed Zionist, became leader of the UK Labour party, and whose first act as leader was to affirm the party's dedication to the Israel lobby and to legitimise the bogus anti-semitism claims against his predecessor and veteran friend of Palestine, Jeremy Corbyn.

Just this month, Labour party officials prevented a party debate on introducing sanctions against Israel, claiming that the discussion "would undermine the party's ability to provide a safe and welcoming space for all members, particularly Jewish members".

UK Labour officials are indeed dedicated to officialising Zionism's usage of secular Jewish identity as a socio-political shield to justify its violent settler-colonialism.

I could not collect my thoughts in time to crystallise one argument before another Israeli atrocity, another airstrike, another court-ordered demolition would take place. Running parallel to all this, as I sat safe from the abject horror of apartheid in England, I was experiencing an intense succession of personal and professional blows in response to the increasing inter-relatedness of my activist and artistic practices, and realisations that many of the people closest to me were only interested in privately expressing solidarity. To be in service to a broader struggle is not a concept that works in tandem with progressive neo-liberalism; extreme individualism is a capitalist ideal that has been re-established for contemporary usage through liberal frameworks that centralise identity politics as the utmost ideological form of activism. I have, as a result, become acutely aware of how that individualism, which in itself is a by-product of colonial arrogance, is used to silence and derail non-participants, such as working-class 'violent' activists and abolitionists, to maintain the status quo where revolutionary action is discarded in favour of visibility politics.

Visibility politics takes a central role in the Instagrammification of activism – as a result, I have always been wary of doing activist work that fits within the parameters of Instagram — this is because I feel that critical political discourse is often discarded in favour of quickly-digestible infographics that can be reposted instantly and forgotten about. However, since Black Lives Matter's radical abolitionist movement went viral last year, activism on social media played a vital role in proving that discursive political thought will not be silenced amidst global lockdown measures. The following paragraph outlines how this played out for the movement for Palestinian liberation and looks into the problems faced by frontline activists in Palestine who used Instagram to disseminate experiential information.

Since May 2021, we have witnessed a massive shift in the online narrative surrounding the Palestinian struggle and Israeli war crimes. This shift towards the recognition of Israel as a violent settler-colonial apartheid state on social media platforms such as Instagram, a platform headed by Israeli-American businessman Adam Mosseri, was coloured by Instagram's well-documented censorship and removal of Palestinian content and shadow-banning (content being unable to reach people), which I experienced on my account after curating a free library on Palestinian texts (tinyurl.com/palestinetexts). Israeli defence minister Benny Gantz spoke to officials at Facebook and Tiktok, urging them to remove pro-Palestine content. The widespread explosive recognition of Israeli hostility on these complicit social media platforms (whose mechanism of oppression is the algorithmic censorship of Palestinian content, even more pointed than that of other platforms such as Twitter), was ignited by Muna and Muhammad Al-Kurd's fearless documentation of the forced expulsion of Palestinians in their neighbourhood of Sheikh Jarrah. Muna and Muhammad have been documenting their experiences living under occupation since childhood, when social media was not as prevalent. This is radical for multiple reasons, one of which being that the Al-Kurds have viscerally opposed the enormously debilitating monopoly of controlled political discourse on Israeli military occupation. They did so by exposing the pervasiveness of Israeli ethnic cleansing that was taking place in real-time in their neighbourhood, all magnified by the use of images and live feeds documenting the intense militarised violence they were subjected to. This served as an unravelling magnifying glass mirroring all the other underway, undergone, and soon to be undertaken, ethnic cleansing programmes (or what is referred to by Israeli apologists as 'population-exchange programmes') that had effectively created and maintained the settler-colonial

Since May 2021, we have witnessed a massive shift in the online narrative surrounding the Palestinian struggle and Israeli war crimes. This shift towards the recognition of Israel as a violent settler-colonial apartheid state on social media platforms such as Instagram, a platform headed by Israeli-American businessman Adam Mosseri, was coloured by Instagram's well-documented censorship and removal of Palestinian content and shadow-banning (content being unable to reach people), which I experienced on my account after curating a free library on Palestinian texts (tinyurl.com/palestinetexts). Israeli defence minister Benny Gantz spoke to officials at Facebook and Tiktok, urging them to remove pro-Palestine content. The widespread explosive recognition of Israeli hostility on these complicit social media platforms (whose mechanism of oppression is the algorithmic censorship of Palestinian content, even more pointed than that of other platforms such as Twitter), was ignited by Muna and Muhammad Al-Kurd's fearless documentation of the forced expulsion of Palestinians in their neighbourhood of Sheikh Jarrah.

Muna and Muhammad have been documenting their experiences living under occupation since childhood, when social media was not as prevalent. This is radical for multiple reasons, one of which being that the Al-Kurds have viscerally opposed the enormously debilitating monopoly of controlled political discourse on Israeli military occupation. They did so by exposing the pervasiveness of Israeli ethnic cleansing that was taking place in real-time in their neighbourhood, all magnified by the use of images and live feeds documenting the intense militarised violence they were subjected to. This served as an unravelling magnifying glass mirroring all the other underway, undergone, and soon to be undertaken, ethnic cleansing programs (or what is referred to by Israeli apologists as

population-exchange programs') that had effectively created
and maintained the settler-colonial project that is the Israeli
state since its conception in 1917, with the signing of the
Balfour Declaration – lest we forget why they are in this
goddamn mess.

May 25th 2021 also happens to be the first anniversary of
George Floyd's murder, and the mass protests his murder
galvanised. I am reminded of how we all watched as
institutional racism in contemporary western life was called
out en masse online last year. After the grief, guilt and empathy
experienced by the collective British social consciousness had
dissipated, what remained of the takeaway? I recall how the UK
mainstream narrative focus quickly shifted from the
extrajudicial killing of Black people to the destruction of
property, the removal of statues of slave traders and colonists
and the importance of maintaining 'law and order'. How
transparent is the racialising biopolitical logic of security?

There are no monuments erected in remembrance of the Black
Britons who have lost their lives to police violence in recent
memory, just as there there are no monuments
commemorating the countless Palestinians who lost their lives,
livelihoods and homes to ethnic cleansing as the world
watched.

What remains is rage. What remains is literature. Those are our
monuments, and we must protect them fiercely. As a
Palestinian, I am forever indebted to Black revolutionary
thought to form my discursive political frameworks. The first
revolutionary text I read was Assata Shakur's autobiography.
That was the text that led me to the works of other Black
Panthers, like Malcolm X, who was a vocal anti-Zionist and

stood firmly in support of Palestinian liberation and against American funding of the settler-colonial project. Angela Davis's text, *Freedom Is A Constant Struggle: Ferguson, Palestine and the Foundations of a Movement,* is an incredibly urgent rallying call for cross-border solidarity in the face of institutionalised racism and state violence. Those texts deepened my understanding of race, political action, and biopolitics as more than abstract concepts and helped me understand my decolonised, radical thinking capacity. Indeed many Black revolutionaries, from Nelson Mandela to the contemporary BLM movement, have been steadfast in their support of Palestinian liberation. The links are apparent: between the settler-colonial roots of the US, synthesised by the enslavement of Africans, and the mass incarceration of Black folk in America, to apartheid South Africa, to the formation of the settler-colonial apartheid state of Israel, consolidated by the expulsion of over 750,000 Palestinians and the ethnic cleansing of over 500 villages in the 1948 Nakba that is an ongoing event until this day.

I am also reminded to be constantly vigilant regarding the imperialist cultural exploitation of struggle narratives. We shouldn't need western discourses to dilute and reassess the realities of the aftermath of western imperialism in the Third World; the social and economic precarities are systematically reframed for western colonial justification. We should be wary of that same mainstream decontextualisation of radical abolitionist movements such as Black Lives Matter – as Palestinians, to justify our existence in a world that has been desensitised to our oppression. Instead, we should focus our revolutionary energies on organising together against imperialism and towards genuine decolonisation.

There is still hope and fight within me, and I hope it is alive within you too.

Glossary

Events (in chronological order)

Ottoman rule: Palestine was captured by the Ottoman Empire in 1516 and remained, save for a brief period of Egyptian rule, part of that empire until 1917.

British Mandate: the British captured Jerusalem in 1917 and assumed control over Palestine formally in 1922. The mandate was officially terminated in 1948.

Balfour declaration: In 1917, shortly after the establishment of the British Mandate over Palestine – and after Zionist lobbying – British foreign secretary Arthur Balfour made the following statement: "His Majesty's government view with favour the establishment in Palestine of a national home for the Jewish people, and will use their best endeavours to facilitate the achievement of this object".

This was a green light for the international Zionist movement to begin its attempts to colonise Palestine in earnest.

Zionist migration: In 1903, there were about 25,000 Jewish people in Palestine, and 500,000 Arabs.

The Zionist movement encouraged Jewish migration to Palestine, and this migration was sanctioned by the British Mandate rulers of Palestine. By 1931 the Jewish population of Palestine was 175 000. By 1941 it was 474,000.[1]

Guerilla war by Zionist militias: From 1931, Zionist militias were set up, demanding a Jewish state in all of historic Palestine. These militias attacked Palestinians and also waged a guerilla war against British troops.[2]

Palestinian revolt: Palestinians rose up against British rule and Zionist immigration in 1936. The revolt was finally defeated in 1939, with the help of the Zionist militias.[3]

Nakba: The term 'al Nakba' (the catastrophe) is used by Palestinians to describe the ethnic cleansing of Palestine by Zionist militias which led to the establishment of the state of Israel in 1948. However, in many western textbooks and historiographies it is described as the Israeli 'War of Independence'.

Approximately 750,000 Palestinians became refugees in 1948,[4] the homes they were displaced from were colonised. At least 418 Palestinian villages were destroyed in the Nakba.[5]

Military rule in Israel: After the establishment of the state of Israel in 1948, the Palestinians who remained there lived under military rule until 1966.[6]

The 1967 War: An attack by Israel against its Arab neighbours – Egypt, Syria and Jordan – that resulted in the Israeli state occupying East Jerusalem, the West Bank and Gaza Strip, as well as Egypt's Sinai Peninsula and the Syrian Golan. The popular mainstream term for this event is the Six Day War, a term which celebrates Israel's supposed military superiority.

Naksa: The Arabic name given to the 1967 war, meaning 'setback' or 'defeat'. During the Naksa 300,000 Palestinians became refugees.[7]

The 1973 War: A coordinated but unsuccessful attempt by Egypt and Syria to win back the territories that had been taken by Israel in the 1967 war. It is popularly known as the Yom Kippur War, but as with the 1967 war this terminology creates a false narrative portraying Israel as the benign defender against Arab aggression. The hostilities paved the way for the 1978 Camp David Accords which resulted in the Sinai Peninsula being handed back to Egypt.

Black September: The name given to the 1970 Jordanian military operation which kicked the Palestinian Liberation Organisation (PLO) out of Jordan.

1982 Israeli attack on Lebanon: The Israeli military invaded Lebanon, attacking the PLO's infrastructure and presence there. The attacks were indiscriminate, killing up to 20,000 people.[8] Israel's assault led to the US-brokered evacuation of PLO fighters from Beirut.

After the evacuation of the fighters, a massacre took place in the Palestinian refugee camps of Sabra and Chatila. Up to 3,500 people were killed by a Christian militia allied to Israel, as Israeli troops looked on.

Israeli occupation of Lebanon: After the siege of Beirut, Israeli forces maintained an occupation of Southern Lebanon. This led to a guerilla war, led by the Iran-backed Hezbollah militia. As a result, Israeli troops withdrew from Lebanon in 1999.

Intifada: The name given to the two Palestinian popular uprisings against the Israeli occupation between 1987-1993 and 2000–2005. Literally translated, Intifada means 'shaking off'.

Oslo Accords: A set of agreements signed in 1993 between the late PLO leader Yasser Arafat and the then Israeli Prime Minister Yitzhak Rabin. The Accords, brokered by the Clinton Administration in the US, were announced with much fanfare to the international community as the first step towards a Palestinian state and peace in the Middle East. In reality, they merely cemented Israel's occupation of the West Bank and Gaza Strip, and legitimised the system of apartheid that Palestinians are forced to endure daily.

The Accords were supposed to be a statement of principles before planned 'final status talks', which never reached any agreement. Thus the Oslo process did nothing to address the problem of Israel's illegal settlements and effectively derailed any attempt to pave the way for the return of the Palestinian refugees scattered across the Middle East.

Palestinian Authority (PA): The Palestinian Authority was established – with extremely limited powers – in 1994.

Disengagement from Gaza: In 2005, after the fierce Palestinian armed resistance of the Second Intifada, illegal Israeli colonies in Gaza were dismantled by the Israeli state, and the colonists relocated, many of them to the West Bank. Israeli troops withdrew to the edges of the Strip.[9]

Split between Fatah and Hamas: In 2006 Hamas beat Fatah in the Palestinian Legislative Council (PLC) elections in the West Bank and Gaza. The Israeli state responded by refusing to recognise the Hamas administration, and preventing the transfer of customs duties to the PA.[10]

Fatah refused to recognise the results of the election, and conflict between the two parties ensued. The fighting resulted in over 600 deaths,[11]Hamas retained control of the Gaza Strip and Fatah took control of the Palestinian Authority in the West Bank.

Since then, the Hamas government in Gaza has faced international isolation and boycott, while the unelected Fatah administration in the West Bank has been backed by the US and EU.

Legislative Council elections have not been held in either the West Bank or Gaza since 2006. In the West Bank, the PA has violently suppressed members of Hamas, as well as other Palestinian political parties.[12]

In Gaza, Hamas has also arrested Fatah members. Both sides have violently crushed any popular dissent against them.[13]

Attacks on Lebanon and Gaza in 2006: Israel attacked southern Lebanon in 2006, killing 1,300 people.[14] At the same time, Israeli bombing in the Gaza Strip killed 416 Palestinians, including at least 135 children.[15]

Siege of Gaza: The economic blockade and military strikes carried out by Israel on the Gaza Strip since 2007 effectively render it an open air prison. Both Human Rights Watch and Amnesty International have denounced the siege as illegal, with Gaza's Palestinian inhabitants living in poverty and shut off from the outside world.

With Israel controlling all but one of Gaza's four borders, and Egypt operating similar policies on the fourth, limited amounts of goods are allowed to pass in and out of the Strip, and 90 per cent of industry has shut down. This has been coupled with targeted Israeli air strikes against factories, universities and schools which are aimed at destroying the infrastructure and institutions needed to build Palestinian livelihoods.

Attempts to break the siege: There have been many international attempts to break the Siege of Gaza. Convoys of vehicles have attempted to bring aid and medicine to the Strip via Egypt's Rafah crossing, and several attempts have been made to break the Siege of Gaza by sea. Some of these attempts have been successful. For example, five flotillas full of aid reached Gaza since 2008.[16] In 2009 a convoy of aid from the UK successfully entered Gaza through Egypt.

In 2010, Israel attacked a Turkish aid ship bound for Gaza, killing ten people.[17] Despite this, international attempts to break the siege by sea have continued, but have failed to reach Gaza.[18] However, several successful land convoys to Gaza have been organised.[19]

2008-9 assault on Gaza: Israel launched a massive attack on Gaza – dubbed Operation Cast Lead – killing 1,167 people, including 318 children. Schools and hospitals were bombed, and the Israeli military used banned munitions such as white phosphorous.[20]

2012 attack on Gaza: Israel launched a new invasion of Gaza – named Operation Pillar of Cloud – killing 171 people, including 34 children.[21] The majority of people were killed by unpiloted drones.[22]

2014 attack on Gaza: The most intense military operation to date killed 2,204 Palestinians, including 526 children in 50 days of bombing during summer 2014.[23]

Jerusalem Intifada: The Jerusalem Intifada – or the Knife Intifada – is the name of the outpouring of Palestinian resistance in 2015-16 in East Jerusalem and the West Bank, which manifested itself in stabbings of Israeli soldiers, settlers and citizens.[24]

Great March of Return: In March 2018, Palestinians began demonstrating at the fence/wall that surrounds the Gaza Strip. Tens of thousands of people participated in the protests, which lasted for two years. The demonstrators were demanding that Palestinian refugees be allowed to return to their lands, and that Israel ends its siege of Gaza. Demonstrators broke through the fence into Israel many times.[25]

The Israeli military responded by firing at the demonstrators with live ammunition, and dropping tear gas from drones. 217 demonstrators were killed, including 48 children.[26]

2021 attack on Gaza and uprising across historic Palestine: In May 2021 Israeli troops opened fire on Palestinians demonstrating against Israeli colonists invading the Al Aqsa mosque compound. Al Aqsa is the third most holy site in the world for Muslims. The attack – coupled with Israel's ethnic cleansing policies in the East Jerusalem neighbourhood of Sheikh Jarrah – provoked rage across Palestine, sparking demonstrations by Palestinians all across 1948 Israel and the West Bank. The military fired on and killed demonstrators. Israeli far-right extremist mobs carried out lynchings of Palestinians in the street inside Israel, and an Israeli settler in the West Bank city of Hebron shot a Palestinian woman dead.[27]

After the attack on Al Aqsa, rockets were launched on Tel Aviv from Gaza. This was presumably just the reaction the Israeli state was intending to provoke, and the Israeli military launched air attacks on Gaza killing 247 Palestinians, including 66 children in just 11 days.[28]

Places

West Bank: The West Bank is part of historic Palestine. From the end of the 1948 war through to the 1967 war the West Bank was annexed by Jordan, and Palestinians living there became Jordanian citizens. It was the Jordanian authorities who coined the term 'West Bank'. The Israeli state often refers to the West Bank as 'Judea and Samaria', names for areas of the kingdom of Israel referred to in the Bible. The West Bank has a population of 3.2 million, including over 410,280 settlers.[29]

The West Bank has been under Israeli military occupation since 1967. Mahmoud Abbas' Palestinian Authority has some very limited control over some areas of the West Bank (see our section below on Areas A, B and C).

East Jerusalem: Jerusalem was divided in 1948, in the aftermath of the war of ethnic cleansing that had been waged by Zionist militias. East Jerusalem came under the control of Jordan until its conquest and occupation by Israel in 1967.

In 1967, the Israeli state annexed 70,000 dunums (a dunum is equivalent to an acre) of West Bank land to East Jerusalem, and applied Israeli law there. In effect, this was an attempt at the annexation of East Jerusalem to Israel. This annexation was against international law, and the territory is internationally considered to be under military occupation. Israel prevents free movement of Palestinians from the West Bank to East Jerusalem, and its policies in East Jerusalem are intended to marginalise Palestinian communities and push Palestinians out.[30] In 2018, US President Trump caused international uproar and protests across Palestine when he officially recognised Jerusalem as Israel's capital and opened a US embassy there.[31]

1948 Palestine (Sometimes referred to by our interviewees as '48 or 1948 Israel): The areas of historic Palestine – amounting to 78% – which were incorporated into the newly created state of Israel when the British mandate ended in 1948, ahead of the 1949 armistice between the state of Israel and Lebanon, Egypt, Jordan and Syria. These lands had been seized during the ethnic cleansing of 1947-9, known in mainstream historiographies as the War of Independence. Prior to the ethnic cleansing campaign Zionists controlled less than 6% of historic Palestine.

The population of the state of Israel now stands at almost 8.8 million. This figure includes at least 1.9 million Palestinian citizens of Israel.

Gaza: The Gaza Strip is a small area of land which is part of historic Palestine. It is around 25 miles long and 6 miles wide, located to the south-west of Israel, and bordering Egypt and the Mediterranean Sea. It is home to more than two million Palestinians. After the ethnic cleansing of 1948, Gaza was controlled by Egypt until 1967, when it was invaded and militarily occupied by Israel. Today it is politically controlled by Hamas, while its borders with Israel are tightly controlled by the Israeli military. This restricts Palestinian freedom of movement and the flow of goods entering, thus suffocating the Gazan economy and causing immense suffering to its people. Although Israeli settlers and troops were withdrawn from the centre of Gaza in 2005, Israel's continued domination of the strip through its military infrastructure on Gazan soil - and constant drone surveillance and aerial attacks, amounts to a continuation of the occupation.

Occupied Syrian Golan: An area in the south-west of Syria which was occupied by Israel during the 1967 war, driving more than 100,000 Syrians from their homes. It is commonly referred to as the 'Golan Heights', a term which ignores Israel's colonial land grab. In 1967, 140,000 Syrians lived in the Golan. Today only 17,000 indigenous Syrians remain, along with 20,000 Israeli settlers.[32] In 1981 the Golan Heights Law extended Israeli law to the occupied Syrian Golan, a de facto annexation which is not accepted by the majority of Syrian residents of the Golan or by international law.[33]

Occupied Palestinian Territories: The Palestinian areas under Israeli military occupation: the West Bank, East Jerusalem and Gaza.

Occupied Territories: All areas under Israeli military occupation (the Occupied Palestinian Territories and the Occupied Syrian Golan).

Areas A, B and C: Under the Oslo agreement of 1993, the West Bank was divided into three zones of control. 'Area A' was supposed to be under Palestinian control, 'Area B' jointly controlled and 'Area C' under Israeli jurisdiction. The agreement was supposed to be an interim measure until the creation of a Palestinian state which would take control of all three areas, save for any areas which were subject to future agreements between the parties. Of course, the agreement never progressed to the next stage, but 25 years later the Israeli state is still twisting the interim measures to its advantage. State policy is to stamp out Palestinian livelihoods and communities in Area C, and give the land to the expanding Israeli settlements. Palestinians are barred from building any new structures, and this is enforced by the home demolition policy.[34]

Al-Khalil: The Palestinian name for Hebron. Al-Khalil means 'friend' or 'the friend of God', referring to Abraham who is thought to be buried there. Similarly, the Israeli term Hebron (or Hevron as it is also known) derives from the Hebrew word for friend.

Since 1968, Israeli settlers have established a number of colonies in the city centre of Hebron, and have launched a campaign of violence against Palestinian residents. The city was separated into two zones of control – H1 and H2 – in the 1997 Hebron Agreement (which followed a massacre by a Zionist at the Ibrahimi mosque). The Israeli military retained control of security matters in H2, which includes a large part of the city centre. 34,000[35] Palestinians in H2 now experience extreme limits on their freedom of movement and intense violence and harassment from the thousands of Israeli soldiers occupying the city.[36]

Jordan Valley: Located in the eastern part of the West Bank, with the southern parts bordering the Dead Sea and the eastern parts bordering the Jordan River. The Valley comprises 28.5 per cent of the entire West Bank and has the most fertile land in the region. It was occupied by the Israeli army in 1967 and is now home to 30 Israeli colonies, around 9 settlement outposts and 24 military bases of varying sizes. The Palestinian population of the Jordan Valley stood at 320,000 in the period between 1948 and 1967, and has fallen to just 65,000 today. Despite the large number of settlements, the settler population is only around 11,000. 95% of the Valley is controlled by Israel for the benefit of industrial settler agriculture.[37]

Israeli politicians have announced their intention to annex the Jordan Valley to Israel.[38] This plan received support from the Trump administration in the US in 2020, although it has currently been shelved.

Al Quds: The Islamic name for Jerusalem, meaning 'The Holy'.

Naqab: The Palestinian name for the desert situated in what is now southern Israel (known as the Negev in Hebrew), covering around 60 per cent of the country's land mass.

Kibbutz/Moshav: Types of Israeli-Jewish collective communities traditionally based on agriculture. The Kibbutz movement was one of the largest recipients of stolen Palestinian land after 1948.[39]

The Green Line: The line demarcating the furthest advance of Zionist troops into Palestinian territory in 1949.

The apartheid wall: The Israeli state began building the apartheid wall inside the West Bank in 2002. It is not built along the Green Line, but instead cuts deep into the West Bank. The wall cuts off Palestinians from their land, and is intended as a massive land grab. In 2004, the International Court of Justice ruled the construction of the Wall illegal.[40]

Gaza wall: Gaza is currently surrounded by a barrier; in some places a fence, in some places a concrete wall, complete with machine gun towers and a security road patrolled by tanks and armoured personnel carriers.

The original fence around Gaza was built in 1994, but was largely torn down by Palestinians at the beginning of the Second Intifada. It was rebuilt between 2000 and 2001.[41] In 2021,

Israel finished constructing an underground barrier along the route of the existing fence to prevent people tunnelling underneath the wall, and is fortifying the fence, building a larger barrier out of concrete and metal.[42]

Gaza marine barrier: In 2018, the Israeli Ministry of Defence began constructing a 37 mile long marine barrier off the coast of the Gaza Strip.[43]

Palestinian refugee camps: Set up by the United Nations Relief and Works Agency (UNWRA) in the West Bank, Jordan, Lebanon, Syria and the Gaza Strip to accommodate the Palestinian refugees of 1948 and 1967.[44] These camps still exist today, although they are more like permanent overcrowded and under-resourced urban neighbourhoods than camps.

Terms

Palestinian-Israeli: Palestinian citizens of Israel. The term 'Arab-Israeli' is commonly used in the mainstream and Zionist media. But the term is often considered offensive, as the term 'Arab' is used in Zionist colonial discourse to negate the existence of Palestinians, and imply that Palestinian Arabs are not indigenous to the land.

Bedouin: Primarily nomadic or semi-nomadic pastoralists who live in the deserts of North Africa and the Middle East. Prior to the creation of the state of Israel the majority of Palestinian Bedouin resided in the south of Palestine, in Bir Saba, the Naqab and south of Al-Khalil. Whilst most of the Palestinian Bedouin were forcefully expelled from these areas by Zionist forces during the Nakba, around 130,000 remain in the Naqab.

Many of those expelled from the south now live in the West Bank, including in Area C communities in the Jordan Valley.

Zionism: An ideology and political movement – whose origins date from the 19th Century – which asserts that all Jewish people constitute one nation, and advocates the creation of a Jewish homeland. The movement is a racist and colonialist one, aimed at creating a state which acts only for its Jewish citizens, and attempts to erase diversity. David Ben Gurion – a Zionist leader in British mandate Palestine who became Israel's first Prime Minister – encapsulated Zionism's aim when he said: "We must expel Arabs and take their place." [45]

Palestinian Refugees: The Palestinians who have been forced to leave their homes since 1948, and their descendants. There are now more than 7.1 million Palestinian refugees worldwide. [46]

Right of Return: One foundation of the Palestinian struggle is that the refugees and their descendants have the right to return home. This right is also guaranteed to Palestinian refugees in international law. [47]

Palestinian refugees have been prevented from returning to Palestine since 1948. The injustice of this is highlighted by the fact that all peoples of Jewish heritage worldwide have a right to citizenship in the State of Israel.

Home demolition: Israel demolishes Palestinian structures at a rate of approximately 450-1000 per year.

Israel's demolitions are concentrated in key strategic areas of planned settlement expansion. Hundreds of Palestinian communities in these areas are under threat of being wiped off the map by these demolitions.

Palestinian communities face home demolitions inside Israel's 1948 borders too. For example, the Palestinian Bedouin village of Al-Araqib had been demolished 189 times as of July 2021.

In Gaza, the Israeli military carries out demolitions of agricultural land and property in the area alongside Israel's wall, which runs along three sides of the Gaza Strip. The Israeli military has declared this area a 'buffer zone,' and does not allow building there.[48]

Targeted assassinations: Israel neither confirms or denies its targeted assassination policy, but Israeli state assassinations are estimated to have killed at least 2,700 people since 1948. Israel's state-orchestrated murders take many forms, but the most high profile are the assassinations that Israel carries out using armed unpiloted drones.[49]

Drones: Israel deploys small remote controlled drones, and also larger unpiloted military aircraft. They are deployed both as surveillance aircraft, and armed with missiles. Thousands of people in Gaza have been killed in Israeli drone strikes.[50]

Apartheid: A term meaning a legal system of racial segregation, originally used to describe the policies of the White National Party governments ruling South Africa between 1948 and 1994. The term is often used by Palestinians to describe the system of racial discrimination established by the state of Israel.

The definition of the crime of apartheid, as defined by the 2002 Rome Statute of the International Criminal Court, is inhumane acts "committed in the context of an institutionalized regime of systematic oppression and domination by one racial group over any other racial group or groups and committed with the intention of maintaining that regime."[51]

Ethnic cleansing: A term which was first used to refer to the atrocities committed during the break-up of the former Yugoslavia. It has been defined as a "policy of a particular group of persons to systematically eliminate another group from a given territory on the basis of religious, ethnic or national origin. Such a policy involves violence and is very often connected to military operations. It is to be achieved by all possible means, from discrimination to extermination".[52]

In *The ethnic cleansing of Palestine*, written in 2006, Israeli historian Ilan Pappe argues that this term can be used to describe the destruction of villages, expulsions, murder and massacres which occurred during the colonisation of Palestine from 1947-9.

The term 'ethnic cleansing' has been criticised by some anti-racists because the term 'cleansing' could imply the presence of impurity. However, 'ethnic cleansing' has become a popular term used by many Palestinians to describe a particular type of colonialism and the actions of armed Zionist groups before, during and after the 1948 war. The term can also be applied to the expulsions of Palestinians from the West Bank during the 1967 war. Smaller scale acts of ethnic cleansing are perpetrated regularly by the Israeli state.

Judaization: the systematic attempts by the Israeli government and settler organisations to move Jewish people into areas populated by Palestinians in order to alter the demographic balance in favour of Jewish people. Judaization is often coupled by the systematic denial of services to Palestinian areas in the state of Israel and in East Jerusalem.

Normalisation: A term used to describe the promotion of economic, cultural and political ties with Israel with the aim of consolidating Israeli occupation and apartheid. US foreign policy is designed to promote normalisation of relations between Arab states and the state of Israel. Most recently US pressure brokered a normalisation deal between Israel, the United Arab Emirates and Bahrain.[53]

Settlement/colony: This refers to the transfer and settlement of an Israeli-Jewish population into the occupied territories of the West Bank, East Jerusalem and Syrian Golan. It covers not only the act of settling in these territories, but is also used to describe the communities which Israeli-Jewish settlers establish.

The Rome Statute of the International Criminal Court defines the "transfer, directly or indirectly, by the Occupying Power of parts of its own civilian population into the territory it occupies" as a war crime.[54] More than 620,000 Israeli-Jewish settlers currently live in the West Bank and East Jerusalem, whilst an estimated 23,000 live in the occupied Syrian Golan.[55] These settlements are not only built on land stolen from Palestinians and Syrians, but they also continually rob nearby local populations of other resources such as water.

However, the Israeli state and Israeli Zionist organisations also pursue a process of land grabs and colonisation within Palestinian areas inside Israel's 1948 borders. This occurs, for example, in the Naqab where state policy and parastatal organisations like the Jewish National Fund are being used to evict Palestinian Bedouins and replace their communities with Jewish-only kibbutzes. In reality there is little difference between Israeli policies of colonisation within Israel's 1948 borders and its settlement policy in the West Bank.

Popular Committees: Palestinian committees which began to be set up in the First Intifada, aimed at creating a grassroots platform for mass popular resistance to the Israeli occupation, carrying out popular education, and building Palestinian autonomy. The concept of Popular Committees have been key to the popular struggle since the Second Intifada too, but the Palestinian Authority has tried hard to control and dominate the Popular Committees.[56]

Popular resistance/struggle: A term often used for the non-military struggle against the occupation. This includes prisoner hunger strikes, the popular struggle in the cities and villages against Israel's apartheid wall and settlements, and the boycott, divestment and sanctions movement.

The popular demonstrations across Palestine are sometimes called the 'non-violent' struggle against the occupation by Palestinians. The 'non-violent' struggle refers to the unarmed popular resistance against the occupation (which is met by extreme armed violence). In contrast to European pacifists' conceptions of 'non-violence', it does not exclude the throwing of stones at Israeli forces, which is a widespread form of anti-colonial resistance in the struggle.[57]

Palestinian movements

Fatah: (meaning 'to conquer' or 'opening') was set up in the late 1950s by Yasser Arafat and Abu Jihad. FATH is the inverted acronym of the Harakat al-Tahrir al-Watani al-Filastini or 'Palestine National Liberation Movement'.

Fatah obtained support from the Syrian state in the '60s, and based itself out of Damascus. It carried out its first military operation against Israeli in 1964 and established itself formally in 1965.

Fatah's initial strategy was a military one, but it has officially pursued a two-state solution since the late '80s, and was the primary Palestinian political party involved in the 1993 Oslo Accords.

Fatah's co-founder – Yasser Arafat – became the first President of the Palestinian Authority in 1994.[58] Fatah is now in control of the Palestinian Authority (PA) in the West Bank, but the PA's authority is extremely limited, the PA's role is essentially to manage the Palestinian population on behalf of the Israeli occupiers.

Mahmoud Abbas became PA President in 2005, after Arafat's death. Abbas has publicly stated that he does not support the right to return for Palestinian refugees (although he later tried to backtrack).[59] On his watch, the PA has collaborated with Israeli security forces[60] and arrested and tortured Palestinians.[61]

Hamas won the PLC elections in 2006, but Fatah refused to cede control to them in the West Bank. Fatah has held unelected power over the PA in the West Bank ever since.

Palestine Liberation Organisation (PLO): The PLO was formed in 1964, and had its roots in the Arab nationalist movements that were prominent at the time.[62] The PLO's stated goal was the liberation of all of historic Palestine through armed struggle.[63] It is an umbrella organisation, which is recognised by many Arab states as the sole representative of the Palestinian people, and which has observer status at the United Nations.[64]

Initially based in Jordan, the PLO was forced to move to Lebanon after conflict with the Jordanian state in the 'Black September' of 1970. In 1982 the Organisation was forced to move again to Tunisia, after Israel's invasion of Lebanon. The PLO's fighters had to remain in military camps in different Arab countries until the conclusion of the Oslo Accords.[65]

Structurally, the PLO is made up of an Executive Committee, the Central Committee and the Palestinian National Council (PNC), which was envisaged as the Palestinian parliament in exile.

Throughout its history, the PLO has been dominated by Fatah.[66]

In 1988 the PLO issued the Palestinian Declaration of Independence, which signified its support for a two-state solution, and called for a Palestinian state to be established within the Green Line.[67]

Popular Front for the Liberation of Palestine: Founded by George Habash following the Israeli colonial occupation of 1967, the PFLP is a Marxist-Leninist communist resistance movement, set up with the aim of guerilla warfare to achieve the liberation of Palestine. According to the PFLP's Strategy for the Liberation of Palestine:

"The aim of the Palestinian liberation movement is to establish a democratic national state in Palestine in which both Arabs and Jews will live as citizens with equal rights and obligations and which will constitute an integral part of the progressive democratic Arab national presence living peacefully with all forces of progress in the world." By the 1970s the PFLP had firmly pledged allegiance to the Soviet Union.[68]

The Front has played an important part in the Palestinian armed struggle, orchestrating several plane hijackings in the 1970s.[69] The group maintained connections with international guerilla resistance movements such as Germany's Red Army Faction and the Kurdistan Workers' Party (PKK).[70]

The PFLP initially joined the PLO, but left in 1993 in opposition to the two-state solution. The Front opposed the Oslo Accords and boycotts the Palestinian National Council.

Since 2000, the Front has made statements accepting the "reality" of the need to accept a solution based on the Green Line.[71]

Democratic Front for the Liberation of Palestine: In 1969 Nayef Hawatmeh and Yasser Abed Rabbo broke from the PFLP to form the openly Maoist DFLP. The DFLP joined the PLO, and has helped to form the PLO's 'two-state solution' stance. The Front has been involved in armed resistance to the Israeli occupation from various bases in Jordan, the Golan Heights and Lebanon.[72] The DFLP provided training to the PKK, as well as Nicaragua's Sandinistas.[73]

The Front declined in influence – as did the PFLP – after the collapse of the Soviet Union, but stood candidates in the Palestinian Presidential elections in 2005[74] and the most recent elections for the PLC (way back in 2006).[75]

Islamic Jihad: Palestinian Islamist movement formed in the early 1980s, inspired by the 1978/9 Islamic revolution in Iran. Jihad means to struggle. Islamic Jihad's aim was to build a bridge between the Palestinian nationalist movement and Islam. The movement has played a substantial role in armed resistance against the Israeli occupation.[76] The organisation is not part of the PLO, and rejects the Oslo Agreements. Islamic Jihad has been backed by the Syrian and Iranian states, although this alliance has suffered since the Syrian Civil War.[77]

Hamas: An acronymn of Harakat al-Muqawamah al-'Islamiyyah, or the 'Islamic Resistance Movement'. Hamas has its roots in Egypt's Islamist Muslim Brotherhood. The organisation was founded as a separate entity in 1987, after the outbreak of the first Palestinian Intifada.[78]

Hamas won the Palestinian Legislative Council elections in 2006, but Fatah would not cede control to them. Hamas retained control of the Gaza Strip, which it has governed ever since.

An economic boycott of Gaza has been in place by European powers, Israel and the US since 2007 – as punishment for electing Hamas – but financial and material support has come from state and non-state supporters globally including Iran, Turkey and donors in the Gulf States.[79]

Internationally, the movement was initially based in Jordan until 1999 when they were kicked out. Hamas then operated out of Syria – supported by Bashar Al-Assad - until 2012, when Al-Assad accused Hamas operatives of supporting the armed resistance against his regime.[80] Hamas currently has an international presence in Qatar and Turkey and close relations with Hezbollah in Lebanon.[81]

The organisation rejects all agreements with Israel, including the Oslo Accords.[82]

BDS Movement: The Boycott, Divestment and Sanctions (BDS) movement is a Palestinian civil society movement, which came together after the international BDS call was made by hundreds of Palestinian grassroots groups – as well as groups representing the occupied Syrian population in the Golan - in 2005, in the aftermath of the ruling from the International Court of Justice that Israel's apartheid wall was illegal. The call reads:

"We, representatives of Palestinian civil society, call upon international civil society organizations and people of conscience all over the world to impose broad boycotts and implement divestment initiatives against Israel similar to those applied to South Africa in the apartheid era. We appeal to you to pressure your respective states to impose embargoes and sanctions against Israel. We also invite conscientious Israelis to support this Call, for the sake of justice and genuine peace. These non-violent punitive measures should be maintained until Israel meets its obligation to recognize the Palestinian people's inalienable right to self-determination and fully complies with the precepts of international law by:

1. Ending its occupation and colonization of all Arab lands and dismantling the Wall

2. Recognizing the fundamental rights of the Arab-Palestinian citizens of Israel to full equality; and
3. Respecting, protecting and promoting the rights of Palestinian refugees to return to their homes and properties as stipulated in UN resolution 194." [83]

The Boycott National Committee was set up to represent the interests of the groups who had signed the call.

Since 2005, the BDS movement has grown into a global force to be reckoned with. Israel's Ministry of Strategic Affairs has mounted international efforts to counter the effects of BDS internationally, and to encourage states to criminalise BDS activity.[84]

1. https://imeu.org/article/the-nakba-65-years-of-dispossession-and-apartheid#the%20british%20mandate%20for%20palestine
2. https://imeu.org/article/the-nakba-65-years-of-dispossession-and-apartheid#the%20british%20mandate%20for%20palestine
3. https://imeu.org/article/the-nakba-65-years-of-dispossession-and-apartheid#the%20british%20mandate%20for%20palestine
4. https://al-awda.org/learn-more/factsheet-on-palestinian-refugees/
5. https://nakba70action.org/wp-content/uploads/2018/04/event_nakba70_418_villages_list-1.pdf
6. https://www.paljourneys.org/en/timeline/highlight/14340/palestinians-under-military-rule-israel
7. https://www.aljazeera.com/features/2018/6/4/the-naksa-how-israel-occupied-the-whole-of-palestine-in-1967
8. "The 1982 Israeli invasion of Lebanon: the casualties". Race & Class (1983)
9. https://www.middleeastmonitor.com/20190815-remembering-israels-disengagement-from-gaza/
10. https://www.middleeastmonitor.com/20190815-remembering-israels-disengagement-from-gaza/
11. http://www.ynetnews.com/articles/0,7340,L-3409548,00.html
12. https://electronicintifada.net/blogs/patrick-strickland/accusations-torture-pa-detains-hundreds-hamas-activists and https://imemc.org/article/59350/
13. https://www.hrw.org/news/2018/10/23/palestine-authorities-crush-dissent
14. https://www.independent.co.uk/voices/commentators/fisk/robert-fisk-lebanon-s-pain-grows-by-the-hour-as-death-toll-hits-1-300-412170.html
15. https://www.btselem.org/statistics/fatalities/before-cast-lead/by-date-of-event/gaza/palestinians-killed-by-israeli-security-forces and https://imemc.org/article/22059/
16. https://www.palestinechronicle.com/boats-reach-gaza-despite-blockade, https://www.freegaza.org/ and https://www.aljazeera.com/news/2009/3/9/aid-convoy-enters-gaza-strip
17. https://www.aljazeera.com/news/2016/7/21/remembering-the-mavi-marmara-victims
18. https://legalcasesagainstisraelattacksoncivilianboatstogaza.wordpress.com/2017/06/03/31-boats-challenge-israeli-naval-blockade-of-gaza/
19. https://www.middleeastmonitor.com/20140220-miles-of-smiles-convoy-to-gaza/
20. https://www.pchrgaza.org/en/4-years-since-operation-cast-lead/
21. http://www.mezan.org/en/uploads/files/17207.pdf
22. https://corporatewatch.org/elbit-systems-company-profile-2/

23. https://www.btselem.org/press_release/20160720_fatalities_in_gaza_conflict_2014

24. https://www.middleeastmonitor.com/20151210-why-the-knife-intifada/

25. https://www.aljazeera.com/gallery/2018/9/27/great-march-of-return-six-months-of-protests-in-the-gaza-strip/

26. https://www.mezan.org/en/uploads/files/15952354571567.pdf

27. https://imemc.org/article/video-armed-settler-kill-a-palestinian-woman-near-hebron/, https://phoenix.coop/2021/05/a-new-palestinian-uprising-against-colonial-oppression-is-gathering-national-momentum/, https://www.middleeasteye.net/news/israel-palestine-night-lynching-crackdowns-death

28. https://www.pchrgaza.org/en/cease-fire-reached-after-11-days-of-iof-aggression-on-gaza

29. https://worldpopulationreview.com/territories/west-bank-population and https://www.btselem.org/settlements

30. https://www.btselem.org/jerusalem

31. https://www.huffingtonpost.co.uk/entry/trump-jerusalem-israel-capital-protests_n_5a278118e4b0c2117626b72d

32. https://golan-marsad.org/issues__trashed/illegal-settlements/

33. http://www.mfa.gov.il/MFA/Peace+Process/Guide+to+the+Peace+Process/Golan+Heights+Law.htm

34. E Egret, T Anderson (Shoal Collective), Resisting the Demolitions: A BDS Handbook (2019) - https://corporateoccupation.org/wp-content/uploads/sites/34/2019/03/resisting-demolitions-ebook-v2.pdf, page 19.

35. https://www.btselem.org/hebron

36. http://www.passia.org/maps/view/73

37. https://english.aawsat.com/home/article/2198431/plo-official-israel-controls-95-jordan-valley, http://jordanvalleysolidarity.org/about-us/the-campaign/, https://www.btselem.org/jordan_valley

38. https://www.middleeasteye.net/news/palestine-israel-annexation-jordan-valley-why-it-matters

39. Ilan Pappe, The Ethnic Cleansing of Palestine (2006)

40. https://www.stopthewall.org/the-wall/

41. https://corporateoccupation.org/2018/06/08/equipment-manufactured-by-european-us-and-asian-companies-being-used-to-fortify-gaza-apartheid-walla/

42. https://www.timesofisrael.com/idf-completes-underground-anti-tunnel-barrier-surrounding-gaza/

43. https://www.middleeastmonitor.com/20180529-israel-builds-marine-barrier-north-of-gaza/

44. https://www.unrwa.org/palestine-refugees

45. https://imeu.org/article/the-nakba-65-years-of-dispossession-and-apartheid#the%20emergence%20of%20political%20zionism
46. https://imeu.org/article/how-many-palestinian-refugees-are-there
47. https://www.waronwant.org/news-analysis/palestinian-right-return
48. https://corporateoccupation.org/wp-content/uploads/sites/34/2019/03/resisting-demolitions-ebook-v2.pdf
49. https://english.alaraby.co.uk/analysis/history-violence-israels-targeted-assassinations
50. https://theintercept.com/2018/08/11/israel-palestine-drone-strike-operation-protective-edge/ and https://corporateoccupation.org/2015/02/19/new-briefing-gaza-life-beneath-the-drones/
51. http://untreaty.un.org/cod/icc/statute/99_corr/2.htm
52. Petrovic, D (1994), Ethnic cleansing – An attempt at Methodology, quoted in Pappe, I (2006) The Ethnic Cleansing of Palestine, Oneworld Publications, p.1.
53. https://www.middleeasteye.net/news/uae-israel-deal-calls-peace-palestinians-citing-deal-century
54. http://untreaty.un.org/cod/icc/statute/romefra.htm
55. https://golan-marsad.org/illegal-settlements/ and https://www.btselem.org/settlements
56. https://www.palestine-studies.org/en/node/1651294 and https://english.alaraby.co.uk/analysis/streets-committees-palestine-united
57. https://www.afsc.org/resource/popular-resistance-palestine
58. https://electronicintifada.net/content/fatah-chapter-closed-creating-palestinian-national-congress/5913
59. https://electronicintifada.net/blogs/ali-abunimah/theres-nothing-new-mahmoud-abbas-and-plos-renunciation-palestinian-refugee-rights
60. https://electronicintifada.net/blogs/ali-abunimah/will-mahmoud-abbas-really-stop-pa-collaboration-israel, https://electronicintifada.net/blogs/ali-abunimah/mahmoud-abbas-collaboration-israeli-army-secret-police-sacred
61. https://electronicintifada.net/content/pa-repression-feeds-flames-palestinian-discontent/11456
62. https://oldwebsite.palestine-studies.org/jps/fulltext/38395
63. https://iris.org.il/plochart.htm
64. http://palestineun.org/about-palestine/palestine-liberation-organization/
65. https://electronicintifada.net/content/fatah-chapter-closed-creating-palestinian-national-congress/5913
66. https://electronicintifada.net/content/fatah-chapter-closed-creating-palestinian-national-congress/5913
67. https://electronicintifada.net/blogs/omar-karmi/elections-or-none-pa-already-obsolete

68. https://electronicintifada.net/content/george-habashs-contribution-palestinian-struggle/7332

69. https://electronicintifada.net/content/george-habashs-contribution-palestinian-struggle/7332

70. https://armthespiritforrevolutionaryresistance.wordpress.com/2017/08/31/a-brief-history-of-the-raf/ and https://autonomynews.org/a-time-for-us-to-follow-on-their-footsteps-palestine-kurdistan-and-the-martyrs-of-may/

71. https://www.bbc.co.uk/news/world-middle-east-30099510

72. https://www.paljourneys.org/en/timeline/highlight/23611/democratic-front-liberation-palestine-%E2%80%93-dflp

73. https://books.google.ch/books/about/Blood_and_Belief.html?id=xlITCgAAQBAJ&redir_esc=y

74. https://electronicintifada.net/content/election-day-polls-open-gaza/5409

75. https://web.archive.org/web/20110807051829/http://www.dflp-palestine.org/english/news_%26_reports/al-badil-list-kicks.htm

76. Hamas: A Beginner's Guide, Khaled Hroub (2006)

77. https://www.al-monitor.com/originals/2019/01/palestine-islamic-jihad-meet-syria-regime-support.html

78. https://www.csmonitor.com/World/Middle-East/2009/0513/p06s19-wome.html and Hamas: A Beginner's Guide, Khaled Hroub (2006)

79. https://www.haaretz.com/1.5176983, https://www.msn.com/en-ae/news/other/revealed-how-a-bank-in-turkey-funded-hamas-terror-operations/ar-BB1amuW4

80. https://www.al-monitor.com/originals/2021/01/hamas-syria-regime-restore-ties-hezbollah-iran-mediation.html and Hamas: A Beginner's Guide, Khaled Hroub (2006)

81. https://english.aawsat.com/home/article/2707636/turkey%E2%80%99s-support-hamas-hinders-improvement-relations-israel and https://english.aawsat.com/home/article/2170977/hamas-new-base-turkey-after-limiting-presence-lebanon-qatar

82. https://www.middleeasteye.net/news/hamas-2017-document-full

83. https://bdsmovement.net/call

84. https://www.theguardian.com/news/2018/aug/14/bds-boycott-divestment-sanctions-movement-transformed-israeli-palestinian-debate